# APPRENTICE TO POWER

# APPRENTICE TO POWER
## A Woman's Awakening

## Jennifer Morse

ACACIA

PUBLISHING
CORPORATION

Published by Acacia Publishing Corporation
23852 Pacific Coast Highway, Suite 756
Malibu, CA 90265

Project Editors: Andrea Cagan, Nancy Grimley Carleton
Editorial Assistant: Claudette Charbonneau
Cover Art: Beth Avary
Cover Design: Lightbourne Images
Book Design and Composition: Classic Typography

Manufactured in the United States of America.

10 9 8 7 6 5 4 3 2 1

Library of Congress Cataloging-in-Publication Data
Morse, Jennifer, 1957–
    Apprentice to power : a woman's awakening / Jennifer Morse.
    p.   cm.
    ISBN 0–9650958–1–9 (trade paperback)
    1. Morse, Jennifer, 1957–    . 2. Spiritual biography—United States.   3. Family therapists—United States—Biography.
4. Shamanism—United States.   5. Andrews, Lynn V.   I. Title.
BL73.M67A3    1996
299'.93—dc20                                          96–15975
                                                          CIP

This book is dedicated to my father,
John S. Morse;
to my teacher,
Lynn V. Andrews;
and to
the Sisterhood of the Shields.

*Acacia publishes books that inspire personal growth and health in heart, mind, body, and spirit, and raise people's consciousness to align with nature and promote planetary healing and balance.*

# CONTENTS

Foreword by Lynn V. Andrews  ix
Preface  xiii
Acknowledgments  xvii

1  Meeting With a Shaman  1
2  Act of Power Ceremony  13
3  Healing Wounds  23
4  A Shamanic Journey  31
5  Target or Arrow?  47
6  Relationship or Capitulation?  51
7  Misadventures in L.A.  63
8  Around the Medicine Wheel  71
9  Commitment Versus Truth  79
10  The Eclipse  89
11  Quickening of the Heart  101
12  Shields to the Four Directions  109
13  Connection to the Primordial  123
14  Pragmatic Shamanism  133
15  Clan of the Whistling Elk  139

16  Crack Between the Worlds  147

17  Living the Goddess?  155

18  Translations  161

19  Sacred Sounds  171

20  Rainbow Mother  175

21  The Help of Unseen Hands  181

22  Taking a Stand  189

23  Lucid Dreaming  205

24  Transitions  217

25  The Anger Doll  223

26  Grieving and Grace  233

27  The Sacred Womb  239

Epilogue  249

About the Author  253

# FOREWORD
## JENNIFER MORSE: AN APPRENTICE TO POWER

BECOMING AN APPRENTICE TO A TRUE PATH OF WISDOM and knowledge is an act of power in itself. To become an apprentice is to be able to honor your teachers without condition, to honor their ability, their knowledge, and their capacity to impart that knowledge to you through energy work and their own life experiences.

To become an apprentice is to say to the Great Spirit, "I give over the distractions, the illusions, and the superfluous activities of my life to a better and more powerful way of living."

Jennifer Morse became an apprentice to power and to me many years ago. She came to me much as I came to my teachers, open about her frailties and the difficulties that she was facing in balancing spirit with her everyday physical world. Becoming an apprentice in the twentieth century is a very different endeavor than it was three thousand years ago, or even three hundred years ago, when an apprentice lived within the mystery school itself, surrounded daily by an environment of learning and higher consciousness. An apprentice within a native, tribal culture was encircled by a tradition passed down for centuries and given to those who were worthy. A world of sacred activity surrounded such an apprentice. Today, however, our lifestyles seem to pull us away from sacred activity, distracting us into the momentary, physical pleasures of life.

To become an apprentice is to set aside what you always thought was your only reality and discover new aspects of existence. You learn to trust and follow new energies and let go of aspects of your life that no longer serve you so that something new has an opportunity to enter into your consciousness.

I've always thought of the astronauts with great respect. I've found it very interesting that many of those who have traveled into outer space, even if only for a few days, have returned having experienced God or Spirit as they never had before. It seems to me that this experience came to them because they were removed from their by-rote lives long enough for spirit and a new wisdom to enter. Many of them have said that coming back to earth was like being reborn—reborn in spirit, not only in the ways they looked at their lives. The experience was transforming because they allowed the unexplainable, the great mystery, and the intangible aspects of life to become real to them.

So, too, an apprentice is faced with a whole new world of archetypes, a whole new world of energy and the challenge of what to do with that energy. The effort we put into the mirrors we see before us will determine if we become masters, shamans, in our own lives.

I have been privileged to work with many committed apprentices who have made various and extraordinary acts of power along the way. Jennifer Morse has written a definitive and honest account of her own struggle along this path to power. I honor her for her integrity and perseverance when lesser people would have turned away. She discovered that the shamanic journey of healing is never ending. Many would have gone back into the seductive distractions of twentieth-century life and hidden away from the change and mysteries that inner growth implies. They would have lost the moment that Jennifer Morse captured: She became the courageous woman she is—a woman who is a true apprentice to power.

Lynn V. Andrews

# PREFACE

I BEGAN MY OFFICIAL APPRENTICESHIP WITH WRITER and shaman Lynn V. Andrews in 1988, but informally, it had already begun. In 1983 when I completed graduate school, the aftermath of a difficult childhood, combined with a relationship falling apart, hit me with so much pain that I fell into a severe depression. A friend, worried about my fragile state of being, brought me a copy of the book *Medicine Woman* by Lynn Andrews. My friend had found it an entertaining story and hoped it would entertain me and maybe even cheer me up.

I accepted the book with disinterest, but once I opened it, I devoured the entire book in one night with an overriding sense that I had come home. To what, I had no idea. I had been searching for a long time with no clear direction. I had completed my master's degree in counseling, gathering an array of theoretical knowledge. I had fulfilled my plan of setting up my own practice to put into action all that I had learned, but something was missing. Despite my in-depth study of psychology and the personal therapeutic work I had done on my psyche, I still felt fearful a great deal of the time, doubting the accuracy of my own perceptions, confused about my point of view, resistant to being responsible for myself, and afraid to take a stand about what mattered to me. I craved a deeper truth than mere counseling techniques could provide. I felt dried up inside, as though I were gasping for a long drink of the magical elixir of life that might quench my thirst for connection to the sacred. I had no idea where to get it until I read *Medicine Woman*.

To my delight, I discovered that Lynn had written a second book, and then, a few months later, a third appeared. I read like one possessed, poring over the descriptions of the events that challenged Lynn's belief systems, attempting to digest the wisdom that her teacher, Agnes Whistling Elk, provided in the form of shamanic teachings. Psychology remained an important component on my journey to wisdom, but with Lynn's books, I was introduced to an unfamiliar yet refreshing approach to self-improvement. I discovered a new meaning for the word *power*. I began to recognize power as an egoless gathering of strength and wisdom to be used for the good of all. I dreamed of ways to combine these sacred teachings with my psychology and to integrate the entire body of wisdom into my everyday life.

In the fall of 1988, I joined a group of women attending Lynn's very first workshop, "Into the Crystal Dreamtime." It was a magical weekend filled with meditations and shamanic practices that paralleled Lynn's own initiation experiences into the feminine aspects of shamanism. While I continued my psychological journey, I furthered my studies with Lynn, attending her yearly retreats, working with her on an individual basis, and joining her school for shamanic studies.

Lynn always made it clear to me that our work together was not psychotherapy. Rather, she was offering me the opportunity to be an apprentice to power. Although I thought I understood what she meant, there were times I nearly stopped the work altogether because the dissolution of all that I had previously looked upon as security seemed too painful. And yet, I continued on, holding my vision of something that would feed my insatiable hunger for truth and wisdom.

This book recounts my search for illumination. It is the true story of an ordinary woman struggling with her self-wounds, fighting to regain a sense of personal power in order to create beauty in her life. This book is a testament that psychology and shamanism need not be at odds with each other. Rather, they are twin trails that can work together as a bridge to wholeness and enlightenment.

The integration of the diverse and rich worlds of intellect and ceremony has served as a major healing force in my life, allowing wisdom, power, and beauty to express themselves through me. As you read my story and find your own way along the path, it is my wish that the same wisdom, power, and beauty may be yours.

Blessings on your journey!

Jennifer Morse
Spring 1996

# ACKNOWLEDGMENTS

I GRATEFULLY ACKNOWLEDGE ANDREA CAGAN FOR her enormous talent as an editor as well as her generosity of spirit, which helped carry this book forward to completion.

A heartfelt thanks to Gary Chapin, Ph.D., for his clarity and support.

To Philip L. B. Scott, M.D., a thanks that words cannot fully express for your unparalleled love and support.

# 1

## MEETING WITH A SHAMAN

I HAD BEEN ANTICIPATING THIS MEETING FOR DAYS. I wanted to be cool and confident, but my legs were wobbling. I looked up at the cabin that corresponded to the number I had written down on a scrap of paper. Squinting from the heat shimmering and glaring off the orange and beige stucco, I lowered my eyes to rest them. When I looked back up, the building had taken on a pink cast. I felt dizzy and grabbed hold of the car door. Something was strange; I couldn't even identify the color of the house. All sense of composure left me. "Jennifer, get a grip!" I hissed aloud to myself.

For as far back as I could remember, an empty, hungry void in the pit of my stomach had plagued me. I had tried to fill it any way I could: with alcohol, tobacco, rich food in front of vacuous television, and fruitless conversations that left me feeling bored and inadequate. None of it had worked. The empty space continued to cry out to be filled until, little by little, the void had deepened into a chasm. I was constantly afraid I would fall in, become hopelessly lost in the labyrinth, and never find my way back out. It felt so bottomless and dark, I tried to ignore it by becoming rigid and impulsive, darting away whenever I came close to the edge. It was like a nameless black hole, filled with nothing but ominous shadows of ghosts and phantoms that were constantly being born and rising up to torment me. I hated this part of myself; I had tried to exile it.

But still it lived on, filling me with anxiety, leaving me shaken and needy. When all attempts at extermination had failed, when I realized that nothing would quiet its call, I surrendered. Then it became my teacher, provoking me to become a seeker. My quest was to name the mysterious longing that emanated from the emptiness. My path was the exploration of the painful wound in my consciousness from which the emptiness originated. This is what got me out of San Jose, bringing me to Los Angeles and to my work with Lynn Andrews, a powerful shaman who would guide me in my investigation.

As I drove toward her house for the first time, meandering through the winding roads of Beverly Hills, overhung with swaying palm trees and spotted with jasmine bushes and red and white bougainvillea vines, I wondered what in the world I was doing here. Obviously, reading Lynn's book about her extraordinary shamanic journeys had brought me here, but could anyone really have done these things? I gazed at the palatial homes with manicured lawns on either side of me, questioning how a young, hip, beautiful woman like Lynn could live right here in tinsel town and still be a powerful shaman. I also wondered what drew me to her.

A clear voice in my mind answered me. "When Lynn talks about her medicine teachers, Agnes Whistling Elk and Ruby Plenty Chiefs, when she describes their behavior and speaks of their wisdom, you feel a kinship with these women. You're connected with them, too." The magnetic pull to Lynn that I had continued to feel since I picked up her first book existed beyond my mundane questions and doubts. It didn't matter where she lived. I was here in answer to a resonance I felt when I read her words about these wise women. It was her description of their strength and impeccability of focus, their playfulness, gentleness, and ferocity, all born out of the truth of each moment. These women were beyond convention and rules; they were the personification of freedom, something I had been seeking my entire life.

I had always yearned for an absolute, living, vital truth that could sustain me. From what I had read about their ever-changing expressions of spontaneity and joy, Agnes and Ruby seemed to embody all that I had been seeking. Without finding it, I knew I would be eternally depressed.

I twisted my way up into the surrounding hills, turning up a side road that looked like an alley. I slowed down, literally inching my way up the narrow road surrounded by houses that were crammed together, oversized for their lots. The homes along this street were not mansions, but the sheer density of the individual dwellings within such a confined space overwhelmed me. The hilly wilderness colliding with this crowded neighborhood was disorienting.

With some difficulty, I turned the car around in the narrow road and parked. I walked up to the wooden plank gate inset into adobe, and pushed the button on the intercom.

"Who is it?" a voice asked.

"It's me—Jennifer. I have an appointment with Lynn," I replied.

"Oh yes. Open the door and come up the stairs."

Adrenaline pumped through me as I pushed back the door to reveal a small courtyard surrounded by various levels of terraced gardens. The heady scent of flowers mixed with the heat increased my dizziness. I slowly walked up the steep staircase, admiring the abundant gardenia and jasmine plants. Beside them, large green leaves supported extravagant bright yellow and orange blossoms. I breathed deeply to take in the wafting fragrances and to try to get my bearings.

I stopped for a moment when I reached the upper landing. My strained nerve endings throbbed, and my muscles shook like Jell-O. I looked with doubt at my moss green pantsuit and the two raw amber necklaces around my neck. I had wanted to look like a "woman of power," striving for a casual but sophisticated look. When I left the house, my clothing had looked fine, but now it seemed all wrong. "Why am I so nervous?" I asked myself. I had no answer.

So here I stood on the red dusty tiles, exactly where I thought I had wanted to be. Now I wasn't so sure. I knocked on the door, tensing my muscles in an effort to look stronger and more confident. I must have appeared quite the opposite when Rosa, the cleaning woman, opened the door. I sighed with relief that it wasn't Lynn. There was still hope that I might gather my scattered nerves before actually meeting her face-to-face. Rosa ushered me into the living room, indicating that I should wait. The interior of Lynn's home had a southwestern motif, and I settled on a white sofa covered in Indian blankets of orange, red, and blue, dividing the room in half. In front of me I noticed an unremarkable coffee table and a fireplace, but what stood out were the objects of power all over the room. Feathers, crystals, and rocks covered shelves and the coffee table, and the chair that was at a right angle to the sofa was strewn with blankets of native designs. Across the top was thrown a luxurious lynx skin. I knew that in the Native American tradition, the lynx was a strong medicine animal. Whoever resonated with lynx was a keeper of the sacred secrets and had the ability to unravel them.

I struggled for composure, meticulously studying my surroundings. I wanted to memorize every detail, but each time I tried to focus on one particular thing, it seemed amorphous. When I turned my gaze away from it, I could hardly remember anything specific about that object. Was my degenerated memory the result of traveling? Was my imagination overworking? Or was it simply the place itself? The more desperate I became to appear strong and focused, the more incapable I felt of gathering my thoughts. Soon, I had practically stopped breathing in an effort to control my sense of unraveling.

"What a lovely necklace!" a clear voice spoke out, startling me. I jumped slightly and turned my head toward the doorway as a bright woman entered the room. It was Lynn; I recognized her from the photographs on her various book jackets. She smiled warmly, sitting straight and tall on the chair opposite me. I felt awkward and self-conscious, suspiciously wondering if her comment about my necklace meant that she expected me to give it to her. I focused on her face, trying to regain my equilibrium. My brown hair and hazel eyes seemed drab and uninteresting compared to Lynn's long, curly blond hair and deep blue eyes, outlined with perfectly applied make-up. Smartly dressed in typical southern California attire, she looked more like a fashion model than an extraordinary woman of power. Her eyes probed me. I wanted to hide, but it was impossible. I felt naked and transparent as I shifted my weight on the sofa, fearful of what she might be seeing about me.

Suddenly my mouth opened, and the next thing I knew, I was pouring out my feelings about a recent relationship that had ended rather abruptly. In a petulant voice, I heard myself say, "He said he wanted a permanent relationship with me and then he changed. He tricked me."

"When you're not trickable anymore, then you won't get tricked," Lynn stated. She seemed aloof and distant, although we were sitting no more than a few feet apart.

My mouth fell open, and I gaped at her. In that instant, I vowed I would learn to be untrickable. A fiery energy passed through my veins.

She continued. "What is the act of power you're work-ing on?"

"Act of power?"

"Yes. An act of power is how you recreate your life in a way that touches you and other people with beauty. An act of power is essential; it provides mirrors for your growth. It reflects back to you who you are—and also who you are not." She thoughtfully stroked the lynx fur that she was now holding in her lap. "When I wrote *Medicine Woman,* my mind used to absolutely fog over. In the process, I saw what a dilettante I was. I had to heal that aspect of myself in order to complete the book." She smiled impishly. "Have you ever heard the story of how Agnes got me to do my act of power?"

I shook my head.

"Well, she tricked me, really. After I regained the mar-riage basket, I returned to Los Angeles."

I had read that book over and over. Lynn was talking about a transformational medicine journey in which she stole back a basket that an evil sorcerer had taken from her teachers. Lynn had a faraway look on her face, talk-ing to herself almost as if I weren't there. "When I got back home, I just didn't feel like I fit in anymore. I kept going back to Agnes and telling her I wanted to live with her and the other Indian women to study the medicine ways. Each time I asked she said, 'No, the cities are where the healing is needed. You belong in the city.'"

Lynn smiled with good humor and continued her story. "One day, when I was visiting with Agnes, when I had given up asking her to let me stay, she surprised me by saying, 'Why don't you come here and live with us?' I could hardly believe my ears. The timing was perfect because my daughter was away at school.

"I was so excited! I went back home to make the arrangements. I quickly rented my house with an iron-clad two-year lease and headed back north to be with Agnes. I arrived in the dead of night to find Agnes sitting outside her house in front of a fire." Lynn leaned forward. "I ran down the hill toward her yelling, 'Agnes, I'm here, I'm here.' When she turned to me, her face was icy and expressionless.

" 'What are you doing here?' she asked harshly, tossing a log into the fire.

" 'Agnes, you invited me to come here and live,' I moaned.

"Agnes stayed remote. 'No, you don't belong here. You're not Indian.'

"I started to cry. 'Go home,' she said. 'Go and write the first of many books about our time together. We live in a time of vision. Let the eagles fly.' "

Lynn sat back in her chair and gave the lynx fur a long, steady caress. I had a strange feeling that I was eavesdropping on her memories. Lynn shook her head slightly and, smiling, continued her story. "By now I was hysterical. I reproached Agnes. 'But you always told me these teachings were secret. Now you want me to write a book! I'm a white woman. No one will believe me.'

"Agnes was firm. She said she wouldn't see me or dream me again until the manuscript was finished. I was crushed by the thought of not seeing her in person or visiting with her in my dreams. She wouldn't even let me stay the night. I was hurt and confused, but the idea of never seeing her again was so devastating, it built the fire within me that I needed to write *Medicine Woman*."

Lynn pierced me with her eyes. "If your picture were on the cover of *Time* magazine, what would the legend say?"

"The legend?" I asked, shocked at her abrupt change of topic.

"Yes, yes," she repeated impatiently. "For example, the legend under my picture might say 'Author and Shaman.' What would yours say?"

I squirmed on the couch. How could I speak out my innermost dreams? Did I even know what they were? She continued to stare at me, waiting for my answer. My mouth was dry. I swallowed hard. "I guess it would say 'Healer and Therapist,'" I squeaked out.

"Good. Now I want you to do a ceremony for your act of power." She described the ceremony for me in meticulous detail. I listened well, grateful that she was doing the talking. After she had finished with her instructions, she said, "Remember, an act of power is the foundation for your higher spiritual teachings. By the way, have you done any inner child work?"

The therapist in me sat up tall. Finally, here was a topic I knew something about. I took off on a lengthy, cerebral explanation of the various approaches to inner child work I had used on myself and my clients. Lynn listened patiently. She looked thoughtful. When I quieted down, she cocked her head, squinted her left eye, and said, "I think your inner child is spoiled. She's been running your life."

Heat surged through me. Indignant, I argued with her, informing her that she wasn't right. She didn't respond. We sat together in an uncomfortable silence. Then she spoke with a calm intensity. "Jennifer, we all have a destitute child within us struggling to be heard and healed. Make a pillow for her, and when she is in pain, comfort her by putting the pillow over your stomach while you visualize yourself holding her. Now let's do a meditation to work with that unresolved tension in your body."

I nodded. My mind and body were reeling when I walked out the door and back down the staircase. Fragments of our conversations whirled through my head; words stood out as if they were lit up in neon. Untrickable. Act of power. Medicine wheel. Pillow. Inner child. Lynn had suggested that I go into silence for twenty minutes each day and that I pray. Were these the tools that would heal my depression?

"I cannot heal you," she had said. "The only thing I can do is hold up a mirror. If you are courageous, you'll look. Then, when you say, 'Yuk,' that's when the work begins. The medicine work of this lifetime is to heal all the unresolved parts of ourselves and put the dark mirror back together again. I think you have the courage."

I had assumed I would feel encouraged and supported from my time with Lynn. Instead I felt raw, broken open, and heavily challenged. Numb, I wove my way down the hill and back into the flatlands. The congestion of traffic fell away as I sped onto Interstate 5. The flat, desolate plains stretched into the horizon. The tension in my brow eased, and a smile suddenly flirted with my mouth, then spread across my face. The next thing I knew, I burst out laughing. Lynn had busted me and I hadn't liked it, but she was right. My inner child *was* spoiled and she *was* the major influence behind my stubborn behavior. I had argued adamantly that it wasn't so, but it was. I was impulsive, I nursed old fears and resentments, and I allowed myself to be immobilized by my emotions, which had caused tremendous difficulty in my life and particularly in my relationships.

As the moonscape surroundings flowed past me, I continued to ruminate, doubting that I could remember the details of the ceremony I was to perform. I worried about that, but what disturbed me the most was the idea of twenty continuous minutes of silence. What if I died from boredom? Worse still, what if I lost the edge and fell straight into the void? Maybe that was the point.

# 2

# ACT OF POWER CEREMONY

I TURNED THE STICK ROUND AND ROUND IN MY HAND. It felt smooth and natural. With a piece of string, I attached the paper to it, on which I had written a list. *Feelings of inadequacy* were the words that headed the roster, followed by *doubting, insecurity,* and many others words that described what I felt I needed to give up. This was my "death prayer arrow" for my act of power ceremony. As Lynn had directed me, I had decorated the stick with beads and feathers of various colors, choosing mostly dark ones to signify the heaviness that these difficult feelings carried with them.

The ocean waves rolled in and out as I shuffled across the hot sand, feeling the coarse pebbles beneath my feet. I breathed deeply as I walked, focusing on the area three inches below my navel, allowing a deeper awareness to enter my "shaman center" as Lynn had called it. She said it was the source of my magic and my creativity, and it seemed that every movement I made began there and continued outward. I was beginning to understand why she called it the shaman center.

I stopped in front of a medium-sized red rock, naturally perforated with a group of tiny airholes. This was to be my rock for the southern position of the medicine wheel. I picked it up, walked to a clear spot I had chosen to set up my medicine wheel, and placed the red rock in the southern direction. I prayed. "Powers of the South, of trust and innocence, home of the mouse who takes things one step at a time: Come here and be with me now."

I continued my beachcombing, this time nearer to the water's edge. A gentle ocean breeze rustled through my hair; it felt good to be in nature, to be setting up my circle, to be engaged in a ceremonial search. A shiny black stone called out to me. I picked it up and placed it in the western position of my medicine circle. "Powers of the West, of death and rebirth, introspection, home of the great dreaming bear who goes within to gain vision, place of mystery and the woman within all of us: Come here and be with me now."

I was invigorated and also a little bit impatient. A critical voice in my head told me I looked silly hunting the beach for plain old stones and rocks that I considered significant. I remembered Lynn's stories of her ceremonial adventures. "You must be intensely focused as you perform your ceremonies," she had told me. "Nothing is ever as it looks, so don't allow yourself to be distracted."

An inner voice admonished me. "You certainly don't have much concentration or commitment to your ceremony if you can be distracted so easily." I placed the voice in the background, brushed my hair from my eyes, and continued my search.

A sparkling white rock grabbed my attention. I reached down to pick it up; it fit perfectly into the palm of my hand. I placed it in the northern position of my wheel. "Powers of the North, of strength and wisdom, home of the buffalo who gave away all that we might live, place of challenges and endurance to meet those challenges: Come here and be with me now."

One more direction to go. I walked to the right of my circle, my eyes glued to the sand beneath my feet. I was attracted to a small yellow rock, the color of the sun. My last stone. I placed it in the eastern position and prayed. "Powers of the East, of birth and illumination, home of the eagle who flies highest, and messenger to the Great Spirit: Come here and be with me now."

My medicine wheel was complete. I entered my circle from the east. I stood in the center, facing the west as I had been instructed, because this part of the ceremony was directed to my death arrow. I had been afraid I wouldn't remember Lynn's instructions, but now that I actually was performing the ceremony, I somehow knew exactly what to do and when. I was pulled to each action. Something inside my shaman center had taken over and was directing me. I had only to breathe, to focus, and to listen.

Now I sang a song to call in and welcome the spiritual energies. As the sounds left my lips, they acted like magnets, drawing power to me. I could feel a potent force beginning to form itself around me. The air flowed gently over my skin, and I welcomed the spirits. I took my arrow in my hand and read the attached list out loud, the thoughts and ideas to which I was bidding farewell. No longer would I allow them to run my life. I was cleaning house. When they and the stick to which they were attached burned to ash, my life would begin again, generated by new and positive forces. I held the matches, struck one, and lit the stick. The paper flared and burned away. I was elated, waiting for the stick to disappear into ashes. But something was wrong. The stick refused to catch fire, and an uninvited gust of wind extinguished the flame. I stood there holding the stick, staring at it, stunned.

It had never occurred to me that my death arrow might not burn. What did this mean? I lit another match and held it to the stick. It went out. I lit another and another and another. The stick remained in my hand; the burned matches formed a pile at my feet. I began to attach a negative meaning to my failure to burn the stick, as if I had destroyed the symptoms but couldn't get to the root of my pain. I glared first at the stubborn piece of wood that would not die, then at the pile of worn-out matches. The stick had to go. I had an idea. I would create a miniature bonfire by making a teepee of the wooden matches and then light them all together. That would make them burn. While I piled them one on top of the other, creating a teepeelike formation, I mentally patted myself on the back for my ingenuity.

With a victorious smile on my face, I cupped my hand around a new match and struck it. Touching the match carefully to the waiting pile, I felt a menacing wind blow up and snuff out the fire. Tears of frustration stung the back of my eyes as I tried again. That stick *would* burn; nothing would stop me from completing my mission. But a new strategy was called for. I lit two matches simultaneously, then three. The wind persisted. The slightly charred stick lived on.

I looked at the box of matches in my hands. It was empty. What would Lynn say about this? Was it a sign from spirit prophesying failure? I sat in the center of my medicine wheel weeping, incredulous that with all of my resolution and determination, I had failed. I glanced around the beach, searching for other sources of fire, for people who might have matches or a lighter, or even a magnifying glass. The beach was deserted. The hot ball of fiery sun in the sky glistened off the water, the white caps resembling diamondlike sparks. Images of fire and heat were everywhere, yet my stick was still intact.

Tears poured down my face while I envisioned endless scenarios in which my death prayer arrow was encased in flames. Fire was all I could see; I was like a thirsty traveler in the scorching desert, seeing a mirage of fresh water. But there was nothing real to quench my thirst, just as there was no real fire to burn the immortal stick. My nose ran; the cold wind stung my face. I talked to myself. "Jennifer, focus on the facts. Here is a pile of used matches. There is an empty box. You have to figure out something." But no answer came. Is this how the cave people felt when they were freezing to death and could do nothing to warm their bones? Was this the degree of frustration it took for them to discover fire? I felt a surge of energy in my abdomen. It felt volcanic, ready to explode. It was like a fire within me. Focusing on my center, riding the heat of my sheer will, I faced the task at hand: how to transfer my inner heat to the outside.

I wiped my nose with my sleeve, realizing once and for all that this stick would not burn. I would have to improvise; I would have to change the ceremony. I hoped it would be all right. I looked at the waves crashing and considered throwing the stick far out to sea. But wood doesn't drown. It would only be a matter of time until the tide would carry it back to shore. There was only one possible way to get rid of it. If it couldn't be cremated, I would have to bury it in the ground. I dug a hole as deep as I could make it, said a fervent prayer to spirit to take the charred stick as my sacrifice, and then covered it over. That would have to do. I uttered some final prayers and walked out of the circle, greatly relieved to have finished that phase of the ceremony. Who would have thought it would be such an ordeal to burn an ordinary dry stick with a full box of matches? Old patterns die hard, I thought, as I made my way up a steep incline to set up a new prayer circle, this one dedicated to life.

I placed new stones in the four directions and stood in the center of my second circle, this time facing the east. This was about birthing a new "me." I let the residual frustration of my previous struggle pour out of my hands, legs, and feet like a muddy stream of water, releasing it into the ground. "Give your pain to Mother Earth," Lynn had said. "She can handle it far better than you can. She will translate it for her own well-being as well as yours." Feeling the dark and grainy negativity fall away, I became aware of how reluctant I had been to give away my pain. I had gone through my life telling myself that my pain would pollute other things, so I had held it tightly within, setting up a false protection for myself and the rest of the world. That illusion was dying. I read aloud a list of ten acts that I resolved to complete in order to create my act of power. In that moment, I knew with certainty that if I took total responsibility for the expression of my life, true power would come to me. Life was offering me the opportunity to manifest my destiny. It was up to me to live my dreams.

I moved back into the routine of my life, slightly concerned that the difficulty I had encountered in my death prayer arrow ceremony would cause me problems. My worries were quickly put to rest. As I devoted myself to placing focused attention on each individual task, unfolding events took on a life of their own. After three months of hard, concentrated work, my therapy practice was filled to overflowing. The force of my newfound dedication was like a fire in itself, burning off negative patterns such as procrastination, doubts, and inadequacies. They were being replaced by new emanations of clarity, strength, and wisdom, their polar opposites. Or perhaps they weren't

new at all. I began to understand that these positive qualities had been there all along, hidden by the negative ones
like ominous storm clouds trying to hide the sun.

The hardest part was just as I had expected. Sitting for
twenty minutes a day in stillness and silence was excruciating, a practice that I dreaded. Some days my mind was
so filled with chatter, and aching with unspoken grief,
I wanted to run far away, but my commitment was
solid. I persisted. Eventually the miracle happened. One
day I slipped into a place of inner stillness. The accompa-
nying release from my usual chaotic distractions dropped
me into my center. From this sanctuary, free-floating as if
in a womb, I witnessed the pandemonium of my life from
afar. From then on, it got easier and easier to meditate
until I began to look forward to my silent time.

I was growing less attached to my moods and more
connected to a sense of being centered. Now it was time
to go to work on the little girl that Lynn had noticed was
spoiled and running my life. I got myself a journal and
began writing. We took turns. She would tell me how she
felt, and I would write back, acknowledging and comforting her. Sometimes when she didn't want to talk, I
would write to her, telling her that I was going to learn
to listen and take care of her. No matter what happened,
I would learn to protect her, to pay attention to her, and
to love her. My intention was to create a loving adult
presence for her, to build her a new foundation that
would serve her needs. Lynn's teacher Ruby called this
adult foundation an "inner chief," someone who would

not be overwhelmed by the child and would love her without capitulating to her demands. As I got deeper into the work, I began to notice that much of my pain was being held within the citadel of this child. She housed my grief, my despair, and the depression that had haunted me throughout my childhood and had threatened to stay with me. It was through these wounded eyes that I often inaccurately interpreted other people's behavior as mean and unloving. It was through these same eyes that, conversely, I could not recognize love and support when they were being offered.

As this wounded child embraced the opportunity to express herself, she became more and more present in my life. I learned to soothe her and actually took pleasure in it. I was reluctant to make the pillow that Lynn had suggested; it seemed silly, and I doubted that it would have much effect. Eventually, I passed through this resistance and did it anyway. I chose a piece of soft pink flannel material and sewed pink ribbon on the four corners. It was fluffy and squeezable, and I often held it over my stomach at night, mentally reassuring my child that I would be there for her no matter what. To my amazement, this proved to be the most miraculous tool of all in the healing process. When I lay in bed, talking to this neglected little girl, soothing her with her own special pillow, I knew that she appreciated having something just for her. But the process went even deeper than her appreciation, touching something mysterious and arcane at the level of my soul.

My first meeting with Lynn had been a strong catalyst for important inner changes. The mirror she had held up to me had revealed my indulgences. I could see them much too clearly now to tolerate them any longer. I wanted to feel good; I wanted to be strong. As I healed myself and focused on my work, my heart opened, and I felt more capable of love. After creating my symbolic medicine circles on the beach, I was now beginning to draw a true circle of power around me, one that had a solid foundation within which I could feel my strength and stand tall.

# 3

## HEALING WOUNDS

SHORTLY AFTER I HAD DISCOVERED THE COMFORT of nurturing my inner child, a new client came into my practice. Vivian was in her mid-forties, a petite woman with deep auburn hair and warm brown eyes. Recovering from alcohol abuse for three years, she was proud of her sobriety, having made wonderful and fulfilling changes in her life.

And yet, she complained of depression. She cried during her sessions, telling me that although she fully appreciated the beauty in her life, she just didn't feel happy. I noticed that when her sessions started, she sat upright with a nice straight back, but as soon as she spoke about her depression, she would shrink down into the back of the chair, looking small and helpless.

One particular afternoon, while her tears fell and she huddled in the corner of her seat, I raised my hand to stop her from talking. I cocked my head to one side, feeling I could see her better from that angle, and I deliberately interrupted her. "Vivian," I said. "How old are you feeling right now?"

Vivian looked startled and answered, "About five or six."

I leaned forward to engage her attention, just as Lynn had done with me. "Do you think your depression has anything to do with your childhood?"

Vivian squirmed like a little girl and looked confused. "What do you mean?" she asked.

I saw that my approach had made her feel threatened. I was being too direct for a six-year-old. I changed my tactics. "How does the six-year-old inside you express herself in your everyday life?" I asked her.

She obviously felt easier because she gave a little giggle. "Well, she picks fights with my husband, and she doesn't want to go to work. I haven't worked at all in the past seven years."

"So she's had quite an impact on your life. I guess she's used to getting her way."

Vivian giggled again and nodded. She was looking more and more childlike.

"Let's talk about the child inside of you," I said. I pulled out a pad of paper and drew a circle. "This is just another way of talking about our personality. Imagine your inner child is in the center of this circle. I call one part of her the adaptable child."

Vivian was rapt at what I was showing her. It was as if the child in her had been joined by an adult and together they were watching what I was doing. "This adaptable child is the part of you that wants love. That's all she wants, and she'll sacrifice herself in a dozen different ways to avoid punishment. She wants to please everybody, but she's just a kid and a lot of times, things don't work out the way she wants them to. You know what I mean?"

Vivian nodded vigorously. "It's true. Sometimes I really go out of my way to please my husband. I make him a special dinner or I put on a new outfit, and he doesn't even notice."

I agreed with a knowing sigh. "That can be really painful for the kid in us." I felt the therapist part of me moving back, as if making room for my own child to come forward to talk with Vivian. I was amazed by her unexpected presence. Before my session with Lynn, I had always viewed this part of me as a burden, something to be kept at bay, someone who was needy and troublesome. But now that I was healing her, allowing her to speak felt like the most natural thing in the world. It seemed that she knew a lot. I had no idea that she could even help me with my therapy practice. "Another layer of the inner child is the rebellious child," I continued. "She's the one who wants to get even. She wants revenge because she's mad about the way she gets treated. Is that the part of you that doesn't want to go to work?"

Vivian exploded in a burst of laughter. "Yes! That's her all right!"

We exchanged smiles. I knew exactly what we were dealing with. This was just like the spoiled child that Lynn had pointed out to me. Her child and mine must have been functioning at about the same emotional level. I drew another circle above and to the right of the first one. "This circle is the scolder," I told Vivian. "She's associated with the left side of the brain. The scolder is the critical, demanding aspect of us. She's the perfectionist who sets up the rules. She's rigid, and most of her sentences include the word *should*. Sound familiar?"

"That's my mother," Vivian agreed emphatically.

"Maybe your mother's voice lives inside of you now. Let's do an experiment. During the next week, whenever you can get in touch with an inner voice, notice who's talking. Don't try to change anything. Just be aware. Okay?"

Vivian agreed. When she arrived for her next session, she had a lot to report. "I can't believe how much the voices are affecting me. It's not like I can hear them clearly—they seem to be just below my awareness—but I can feel them in there, and they're influencing everything I do."

We spoke about different techniques to talk with the inner child. I suggested speaking in ways that were loving and supportive, using a kind voice and certain words that would result in acceptance instead of defensiveness. I impressed upon Vivian how important it was to listen to the child and, at the same time, not to capitulate to her demands. "Remember," I told her, "that child is way too young to be running the show. It would be as if all the different parts of you are sitting on a bus and this little one is at the wheel. She can barely see over the steering wheel, her feet have trouble reaching the pedals, and she's driving like the devil is chasing her."

Vivian laughed. "I can just see that bus swerving around. It feels like my insides a lot of the time." Vivian agreed to write in her journal using her inner voices so that she could reread their words at a later time to deepen her understanding. She really wanted to feel better.

Vivian came back regularly and reported her progress. She was amazed at how much the child was willing to share with her, how much she had suffered from being hurt, silenced, and ignored. Vivian felt comforted that she could heal this part of herself, and it was clear to both of us that she was on the path. Her relationship with her husband was improving, and she was beginning to consider some different work options in which she could make a real contribution and be fulfilled. Each time she came to see me, she felt more and more on track with herself, and her depression was lifting.

One day when Vivian arrived, her body looked tense and rigid. She sat on the edge of her chair. "I didn't want to come today," she told me.

Her anger was so close to the surface, I simply nodded, not wanting to disturb the moment or stop whatever was about to happen by speaking.

Vivian looked at me through a dark cloud, her brow furrowed. "My inner child is upset about something, but she won't tell me what it is. I know it has to do with a neighbor I used to have, and it has something to do with swimming. I feel furious, but I don't know why."

"Let's go back. Tell me what you see when you picture that neighbor," I suggested.

She sat back in her chair and closed her eyes. "It's hot. It's summer, and we're on vacation at the lake with some friends. We used to go there on weekends sometimes. Jim is the neighbor there. He's taking me swimming and I'm so excited." Her face lit up. "We're playing in the water. My mother doesn't want to go in because it's too cold." A frown suddenly came over her face, and she huddled into the back of the chair. "I'm scared," she said.

The tension in the air was so thick, I could feel it. Vivian's body was tense and her eyes were slightly open but unfocused. Choked sobs began to rise up in her throat, and she made sounds as if she were drowning. Her body convulsed. "He's touching me," she sobbed. "I want him to stop, but I'm afraid I'll go under. I can't do anything." She held her head in her hands and wept. I wanted to cry, too, for the betrayal and the loss of the innocence of that beautiful child.

I stayed silent, waiting for her crying to come to a natural end. She eventually lifted her head and looked serenely into my eyes. She was radiant, and her face was clear. I looked back at her through the haze of my own tears. "Vivian," I said. "That's something to cry about."

Vivian nodded. "Now I know why I've had such a hard time with intimacy. I didn't even know this had happened, but it's a beginning for me, an opportunity to understand the truth about my past."

It was an opportunity for me, too. Because of my work with Lynn, I was able to help clients like Vivian. I told her how to make a pillow for her child, how to place it over her stomach, and how to hold it as if it were a newborn baby. Vivian didn't resist it as I had; she was already wide open and knew that she needed some tools to help her get through this next phase.

Vivian continued to nurture her inner child. Within six months, she was well on her way to healing herself and beginning a new life devoid of depression. I was proud of her and happy for myself. Because of Vivian's courage and openness, I could find the same courage to delve more deeply into my own truth. This was the kind of focus I had always been looking for. This was the way in which I wanted to give what I had been fortunate enough to receive. My work life was coming together.

# 4

## A Shamanic Journey

I HAD BEGUN MY PRIVATE PRACTICE WITH THREE clients and an unswerving conviction that this was the right path for me to follow. It had paid off. Now that my business was riding on its own momentum, now that I had some degree of inner peace, I could focus my attention on other areas of my life.

As a therapist, I was familiar with all the current "buzz words" of a lasting relationship: *good communication, solid commitment, compromise, shared values.* But for me, judging by my personal experiences, these were only hollow words. I had never had a successful relationship with a man. I encouraged my clients to face their fears about men and commitment, I helped them strengthen their faith in the possibility of creating a successful partnership, but deep down inside, I secretly did not believe a mutually satisfying, nourishing union to be possible. Maybe for others in certain rare cases, but not for me.

Still I wanted it, and the dream of a loving relationship in my life persisted. In this area, I was traditional. I wanted a husband and children. I wanted a life that would allow me to integrate into the fabric of society in a positive way.

Maybe now that I was not so depressed, I could change my belief that I was incapable of finding happiness with a man. I certainly wanted to try. Through my ongoing sessions with Lynn, I had newfound hope and confidence in myself. It was difficult to explain in words how the spiritual work had changed my life, but it was clear that it had. Why couldn't a caring relationship and a family also take form out of this nebulous and mysterious arena of spirituality?

Richard was an unusual combination of reserve and openness. He was a psychologist, and we had had offices in the same building for the last two years. I had seen him coming and going, had passed him in the hallways and nodded hello and good-bye. That was the extent of it. Although I found him attractive, I had stayed remote. After one brief affair that had left me bitter and disappointed during those years, I had withdrawn from having a relationship and concentrated on my business and my inner development. I read all the popular books on the women's movement and the corresponding men's movement. I also questioned my men friends about their feelings and their needs. "What do you want?" I would ask. "What do you think women want?"

I listened to their responses, hungry for information, surprised by their answers, and amazed at how little I knew. I was confused about men, a situation I judged as appalling for a practicing therapist, a woman who ultimately wanted marriage and a family. I was afraid of men; they were an enigma to me. Distant, aloof, powerful, focused, driven. This was the language I used to describe them, along with competitive and unavailable.

In my past relationships, the beginning stages were always great. The men were warm, sensitive, and attentive. But after the initial bond had formed, after the passion had cooled, the relationship would invariably take a disheartening leap into boredom, eventually deteriorating into an empty connection devoid of kindness or affection. From all the information I had been gathering recently, I decided that maybe it wasn't all their fault and that maybe I had evaluated male behavior incorrectly. Much of what I had interpreted as uncaring could have been in fact, something else. Most men had a tendency to become so highly involved in the outside business world that their apparent neglect might simply be an absorption in a task that had nothing to do with me.

One afternoon, Richard and I happened to step into the elevator at the same time. I spoke up. "Would you like to go to lunch with me?" I asked in a strained voice.

He looked straight at me, slightly surprised, and then smiled. "Sure, that would be great," he answered. "How about tomorrow?"

"Good," I said. I exhaled, happy to have been accepted and, at the same time, scared of what I was getting into.

I passed through my fear barrier by meeting with Richard under the guise of investigation. I viewed him as a research project. After all, we were both therapists. I could ask him questions about the male perspective without appearing invasive or inappropriate. He certainly must know more than the average man, having studied relationships for his work. It never occurred to me that since I lacked knowledge in this area, another therapist might be in the same position.

"Are you in a relationship?" I asked him tentatively over sandwiches.

"No. I was, but we broke up a while ago. Since then, I've been pretty active in the men's movement."

A good sign. He was single, and we had studied the same things. We talked nonstop, well after the plates had been cleared from the table. Richard appeared contemplative. He thought about things before he answered. I liked that. Our conversation flowed with ease; his skill at communication delighted me.

"I like to write," he said. "It helps me to clarify my feelings and to grow." I used writing for the same purposes. The more I listened, the more impressed I became with Richard's ability to articulate his thoughts. He was a master at words, describing the subtle nuances of his perceptions with precision. I felt a tingling excitement as I listened to him. I didn't know much about this man, but he certainly was saying all the right things. My own grasp of these concepts had been born out of deep internal contemplation. Surely Richard must have done the same degree of personal exploration. How else could he so beautifully describe this world of ideas that we clearly shared?

Over the next couple of days, I dismissed the tugging feelings I was having about him, mostly out of fear. I dreaded getting involved in yet another potentially heart-breaking relationship. It was easier just to forget it. I did this so successfully that when the phone rang, I was surprised it was Richard. As soon as I heard his calm, well-mannered voice, the butterflies in my stomach started fluttering.

"Hi, Jennifer. I thought you might like to join me for a movie this weekend."

I accepted instantly, but after I hung up the phone, a foreboding began pulsing in my stomach. From there it traveled into my nerve endings and seemed to fire off sparks. I began to sense an alarm going off. I had never felt anything like this. Was this an omen that we were destined to be together or a warning not to proceed? I had already accepted the invitation, and I really wanted a relationship, so I tried to rationalize my way out of it the way only a therapist could. This was probably just the normal tension of dating or an offshoot of my unresolved fears of intimacy. I felt off center and scattered. The only thing I knew for sure was that being in a relationship had never been easy, and apparently this was not going to be an exception.

Mid-week before the movie date, I was scheduled for a meeting with Lynn in Los Angeles. Auspicious timing. The scenery on Interstate 5 reminded me again of a brownish moonscape as I listened to educational tapes: Elisabeth Kübler-Ross on life, death, and transition, a tape on how to communicate effectively in relationships, another on increasing financial prosperity through emotional well-being, and finally, a double cassette by Lynn on practical wisdom. I felt efficient, like a workshop on wheels, speeding down the freeway, trying to take in as much knowledge as I could as quickly as possible. I fell into a kind of hypnotic trance, especially when I did some breathing exercises for the last part of the trip. I wanted to arrive at Lynn's door peaceful and centered this time. I hoped she would see how different I was and how much I had grown.

There was road construction in the hills along my regular route to Lynn's house, so I took some alternate streets. I wasn't sure where I was going, and pretty soon I discovered I was lost, confused, and disoriented. I searched for familiar streets and landmarks, torturing myself with thoughts of missing the appointment after such a long drive across the state. When I finally arrived at Lynn's door fifteen minutes late, my stomach was churning. Data from the various tapes I had been hearing ran round and round in my head like hamsters on a treadmill, getting nowhere, making no sense, scrambling my mind. Despite my careful preparations, here I was at Lynn's, once again in a state of disarray.

I sped up the stairs to the entryway two at a time, painfully hitting my toe as I yanked my feet out of my shoes. I grimaced and placed my shoes beneath the wooden plank. The next thing I knew, Lynn was standing in front of me, ushering me through the hall into the living room.

"I'm so sorry I'm late," I apologized breathlessly.

"You're not late. You're right on time." Lynn spoke warmly, trying to console me.

"No, no. I'm late," I argued.

"You're right on time," she said firmly, her voice taking on an authoritative tone that would not tolerate an argument. She took my arm, led me back through the entryway, turned her back to me, and walked away. She was giving me a chance to arrive again, this time with a different attitude. I paused and took a breath, trying to collect myself. When I looked at the wall next to the entrance, I noticed a massive painting of a chocolate brown stallion standing on his hind legs covering the entire area, floor to ceiling. I didn't remember it. Had it been done since the last time I was here?

I walked back into the living room on my own, still unclear about why Lynn said I was right on time. My watch absolutely told me I was late. Could she have been talking in cosmic terms? The more I wondered about it, the more confused I felt. I sank into the couch, amazed at my instantaneous transformation from professional counselor to awkward neophyte in the space of a few minutes. Whenever I entered Lynn's world, and particularly in her physical presence, all of my training and knowledge flew out the window. It literally held no weight.

Lynn lit a sprig of sage and blew the smoke toward me. I stood somewhat unsteadily. Brushing a large, fluffy owl wing in a downward motion, she wiped clean the entire area about six inches away from my physical body. "Your aura looks good, honey," she said lightly. "What color do you think it is?"

I hesitated, not wanting to give the wrong answer, wishing she hadn't asked. "I don't know," I stuttered.

"Make a guess," she encouraged.

I closed my eyes and tried to concentrate. I decided to make a wild guess. "Purple?" I said tentatively, certain I must be wrong.

"Right!" she said. "It's a beautiful purple."

I looked to see if she was patronizing me. Then I remembered who I was dealing with. Lynn didn't patronize. A feeling of pride washed over me. Maybe I had some hidden abilities after all. I began to relax, making my way around the coffee table and sitting back down on a corner of the couch. The weave of the blankets beneath me was soft and smooth; I soothed myself by touching the orange parts of the colored designs.

Lynn's blond hair fanned outward, surrounding her face like a halo. She sat upright at the edge of her chair, looking weightless as a bird lit on a branch, poised for flight. The flowery pattern on her wool skirt blended in a variety of bright colors, her blouse matching the deep blue tones. "Now, what do you want in your life?" she asked. The session had begun.

I sat up straighter. Her bearing was so demanding of my complete attention, I began moving into a centered state in spite of myself.

"I want a relationship and a baby," I said. My voice had taken on a dreamy quality, and I could hear a longing, ancient and despairing, revealing the part of me that regarded my dream to be an impossibility.

"Good. Let's work on that." Lynn was firm and energetic. "But, Jennifer, before we focus on your outward
relationship to men, I see an imbalance in your male
aspect, the masculine part of your spirit." Lynn cocked her
head to the right and looked at me. "Do you know what
I mean by that?"

I nodded my head a bit dubiously. "Are you talking
about Jungian psychology in which there are male and
female dimensions that sometimes influence our behavior?
And the main part of our personality doesn't even know?"

"Not exactly. In shamanism, the feminine is the part of
us that is about connection, and it carries the void, the all
receptive. The feminine is entwined in Mother Earth, the
giver of life. The masculine part of your spirit is specifically associated with outward worldly things and your
father energy. Our fathers did the best they could, but at
times they didn't meet our needs. That left us feeling
incomplete."

Her words struck a chord in me. I wondered if my
feelings of emptiness and lack of understanding with men
came from this very imbalance she was describing. I felt
these aspects of maleness like restless, unruly tribes, pacing back and forth, calling out for attention. Lynn was
staring at me, her head cocked slightly to the right so that
only her left eye focused on me. Her face took my breath
away; her inner and outer beauty appeared so perfectly
integrated.

"What gifts has your father given you?" she asked
while her hands moved lightly through the air, gently

hovering across unseen places in front of her and then retreating. I was mesmerized by her movements, marveling at the fluttering sensations they caused in me. Her eyes now held a fierceness, a predator quality that provoked me into staying alert.

"He paid for my education. That was an enormous contribution to my life. And he taught me by example how to manifest dreams and ideas into substance. He has always had the ability to persevere and focus on the task at hand, whether or not he has an interest in the project. His commitment always sees him through."

I explained this in a rush and then sat back to contemplate the difference between my father and me. I required a sustaining interest in a project to keep up my enthusiasm to see it through. I always had assumed that my father's approach being so different from my own was a reflection of our different temperaments. We could never quite understand each other, but now I saw a new possibility. Perhaps my father's strength to endure unpleasant tasks was a product of his impeccable spirit and the great force of his intent. Perhaps it was a kind of adult behavior I had not yet embraced. I shuddered as I glimpsed a scattered trail of my past unfinished work. Maybe my own lack of direction and commitment to menial tasks was an imbalance in me created by the child running the show.

Lynn had been watching me carefully, and now she leaned forward in her chair. "Close your eyes," she commanded, "and put your awareness in your shaman center." In one smooth motion, she deftly tucked her legs beneath her. "Now, with your intent, I want you to become aware of a masculine energy around you." Her voice softened. "I sense warmth that he's sending to your heart. This masculine father presence has been trying to nurture you for your whole life. He never will abandon you." Her words became dreamy and swirled around me, entering my belly as if they were wisps of air blowing through me. I felt hollow and transparent.

"See if you can get an image of him, Jennifer. He has great strength and wisdom." Lynn became quiet, allowing me to drift for a while before she continued. "This father presence is not authoritative or critical. His only job is to love you. See if you can visualize him. He is not too old, but you can tell by his bearing that he has resolved the riddles and complexities of life. He can help you do the same. Try and discern his nationality. Is he wearing old-fashioned, futuristic, or perhaps traditional clothing? Get a picture of him as best you can."

I hardly knew if I were awake or asleep, if Lynn were actually speaking, or if her words were providing me with psychic suggestions. Suddenly an influx of heat entered the right side of my body and settled in my heart, softening me. Tears filled my eyes. Waves of joy passed through me. My blood raced; my cells were dancing. I surrendered to the waves, feeling safer and more protected than ever before.

A vivid image of a man in aboriginal clothing filled my inner mind. He stood motionless, holding a primitive-looking spear, the picture of dignity and strength. I felt that he had deep concern for me, that he loved me. I was grateful that he was with me. I could tell he had traversed the trails of power and wanted to share his wisdom.

"Jennifer." Lynn's voice cut through my consciousness. "Find the place in your body where relationships live and tell me what you see."

I searched through my body. My awareness settled on my stomach. "I see a gorgeous rainbow," I told her.

"Become one with it. Hear its message."

I merged with the rainbow. Colors bombarded me, flooding through me until I was every color, every vibration. The rainbow covered the entire inner vision of my mind. It *was* my mind. Then it spoke. "I am the reflection of how you act in relationships. Sometimes I am vivid," it said as a surge of brightness nearly blinded me, "and sometimes I am vague." The colors dimmed. "I am never the same, and my vagueness never lasts. I always leave you hopeful."

It was accurate. My relationships were passionate, and they usually left me lonely but never hopeless. They made me aware of so much love and beauty, but I never could find a way to express these feelings. And I always wanted to keep trying.

"When you are finished with the rainbow, release it from your body," Lynn said at the exact moment the message was over. I marveled at her ability to be right there with me, in tune with each of my visions. I said a prayer of thanks and sent the rainbow off into the clouds.

I was weary from the exertion, but Lynn was not finished with me. "I know you're tired, but we have a little more work to do. Just breathe for a few minutes," she said. I inhaled deeply, fighting my fatigue, determined to stay with my teacher and myself.

"Now focus back into your center," she instructed after a few minutes. "Move your consciousness into your heart. We are going to create a beautiful room, right in the center of your heart. What color do you see?"

"Yellow," I said, without hesitation. "A soft, creamy yellow."

"Good. Yellow is the color of hope and will. Now tell me what you see in your room."

My tiredness fell away. I looked with my mind's eye at the etheric layers rolling and undulating, then taking form into clear, solid objects, glimmering with light. I was in awe as I began to describe the room to Lynn. "I see a four-poster bed with yellow sheets and a down comforter. It's a pale buttermilk yellow. In the corner is a fireplace, filled with wood and kindling." I smiled. I had always wanted a fireplace in my bedroom. "In front of the fireplace is a sofa covered in a kind of raw, bumpy silk, with pink fluffy down pillows."

The images were becoming more and more distinct. They flew together as if I were thinking them into form. "There's a dark, burnished mahogany coffee table covered with books and magazines, right in front of the sofa."

"What are you doing now?" Lynn asked softly.

"I'm curling up on the sofa. I have never been so comfortable. The walls are soothing—a soft pale pink. I love pink. And the floors, they're shiny hardwood. I see Oriental carpets with intricate designs. Wait—they're yellow and pink, too." The scent of stargazers and tuberoses drifted across the room. "Somebody has placed the most exquisite arrangement of flowers on the table. They're my favorites."

One wall of my inner room was entirely sliding glass doors, floor to ceiling. Just outside the doors was a sun-filled deck, partially shaded by towering oak trees. Acorns lay on the deck. The sun warmed the branches of the trees, which cast delicate shadows on the floor and walls of the room. I suddenly felt that, from my seat, I could physically touch the oak trees. "It's as if the trees are reaching right through the doors into this room. They're part of the room. Lynn, this is a tree house!" I exclaimed.

"Jennifer, this is your heart. Open the door to this room in your heart, and see the warrior who is your mate. He is standing at the threshold. Don't be surprised if you can't make out his face. Don't even try. Just invite him into your room."

As I looked to the threshold, there he stood. He was magnificent, the energy waves around his body shim-mering and glowing as if he were made of spun gold. His body was strong, his hair dark, his clothing soft and invit-ing. When I tried to see his face, it was like liquid, shift-ing and changing shape. I resisted the impulse to solidify it; I invited him in as he was. There we sat together, feel-ing each other's presence in my heart space. Our energy appeared in crisscrossed luminous fibers that glowed brightly, especially where we physically connected.

I had no idea how much time had passed when Lynn's voice floated into my awareness. "It's time to come back."

I felt a sadness, a reluctance to leave this newfound paradise and the soul mate who was sharing it with me.

"Don't worry, honey. This is yours now. Just remember to keep the door to the room in your heart open. In order to have a relationship, you must have 'room.'"

As I was bidding farewell to my warrior, I suddenly heard a strange sound. "Wait!" I said. "Do you hear that? It sounds like a baby crying."

"Yes, I hear it."

"Does one of your neighbors have a baby?"

"No, there are no babies on this street."

I said nothing more about it. We had both heard it. That was enough.

When I opened my eyes, Lynn was sitting at the edge of her chair, her legs neatly tucked beneath her, exactly as she had been when we started the session. She swayed almost imperceptibly from side to side, and with a faraway look in her eyes she said, "I see a male figure around you. Stay open to men if this current one doesn't work out."

I nodded, relieved that the visualization had gone so well, that I hadn't learned anything terrible about myself. Over the next few days, my conscious mind couldn't seem to hold onto the specifics of the session, but the feelings remained. I was excited about the prospect of having a mate and a family, and for the first time in years, I believed that it was possible for me. I daydreamed about Richard. I tried to stay open to other men, but I couldn't resist building an imaginary future life with Richard. I discounted Lynn's warning; I began to refuse considering the possibility that he was not the man for me.

# 5

## TARGET OR ARROW?

NED WAS IN HIS MID-THIRTIES, A TALL HUSKY MAN with a round face and blondish hair. He seemed resistant to being in my office, complaining that although he had been in therapy for years, his life was still unmanageable.

I tried to put him at ease during our first session by asking him to talk about himself. He was long-winded; his stories were about flitting from career to career, never quite finding the courage or the interest to make a commitment to anything in particular. I could tell that he was gifted and intelligent by the way he articulated his thoughts. But he had little focus. He jumped from topic to topic with no connecting threads. Recognizing that we were drifting, I interrupted his monologue.

"So what do you make of all of this?" I asked him. "Why do you think nothing holds your interest? What do you think is stopping you from having goals and achieving success in your life?"

Ned shrugged. He had no answers. He looked to me as if it was my turn to talk. I decided to try sparking his interest with a story.

"My teacher was tricked into becoming a writer."

He perked up.

"It had always been her dream to write, but she had never devoted any time to it. One day her teacher, a Native American shaman called Agnes Whistling Elk, asked Lynn to come and live with her on the reservation. Lynn had wanted this for a long time; she wanted to be close to Agnes so they could continue their ceremonial work together. But wait until you hear what Agnes did!"

I paused a moment to make sure Ned was still with me. He was all ears. "Lynn leased her home and generally undid her life so she could stay away for a while. But when she arrived at the reservation, Agnes wouldn't let her stay. Not only did she make her leave, she told her that she wouldn't even communicate with her until Lynn wrote a book about their work together. I guess she knew Lynn's secret dream, and she also knew her resistance. That was the way she knew she could inspire Lynn to go for it."

Ned looked thoughtful. He was considering Lynn's situation and how it related to his own.

"So what would it take for you to focus your intention?" I asked him. "What would it take to turn you into the person you want to be? Agnes used to ask Lynn, 'Do you want to be the target or the arrow?' Do you understand what this means?"

"Yes. I think it means: Do I want to just stand here and be pushed and shoved by whatever comes my way, or do I want to be responsible for my own destiny?"

"That's exactly what it means. It also means: Do you

want to create the direction and move toward your goal
of your own accord? So I'm asking you the same question. Target or arrow?"

Ned squirmed with discomfort. He was being challenged, and he felt the pressure.

"Ned, if you could do anything at all, and I mean anything, what would it be?"

"I'd sell antique cars," he said without hesitation. His
dream was right there on the surface. He didn't have to
dig at all. That was a good sign. He went on. "I really like
to talk to people. And I really like old cars. They're my
hobby. It would be great to match up people with their
dream car." He smiled broadly. "I'd get a real charge out
of that."

I was delighted. "Great! You have the first part of the
dilemma solved. That's the part that usually gives people
the most trouble. You already know what has meaning
and aliveness for you. Now, the second part. Where will
you find the courage to follow that dream, to concentrate
on it and make it happen?"

Ned's face fell. "I guess it's not a very practical dream."

"Wait a minute. How did we get from finding courage
to condemning your dream as impractical in one breath?
Are you giving up that easy? Who told you your dream
wasn't practical?"

Ned became pensive and retreated briefly into silence.
"Friends. Family. Mostly my father. He wants me to be
an engineer."

"What do you want?"

"I don't think anybody ever asked me that before. I want to work with antique cars, but I don't want to disappoint my father."

I understood. Ned had a good heart; he wanted to please his father, but he had to find the courage to live for himself or he'd never be happy. "Ned, I want to talk to you about doing a ceremony. Have you ever done one before?"

He shook his head.

"Would you be willing to try something new?"

"If you think it would help. I'm ready to make some changes, and I'll try whatever you suggest."

"Good. You're halfway there." I explained to Ned about the act of power ceremony. I told him about the prayer arrows, the medicine wheel, the rocks, the fire—all the different elements that make up a complete ceremony. As he left the room, I thought about my incident with the matches and the stick that wouldn't burn. I wondered how it would go for him.

When Ned returned the following week, he was jubilant. He had had a powerful experience. He had received exact information about how to proceed, and he explained to me in great detail the steps he was about to take to realize his dream. I was happy for him, proud of how well he had performed his first ceremony. If his focus and success concerning the ceremony were any indication of things to come, Ned was about to transform his future. He was going to be just fine.

# 6

## RELATIONSHIP OR CAPITULATION?

WORK WAS SAILING ALONG. MY RELATIONSHIP WAS a different story. It's not that it was going badly. Quite the opposite. Richard and I were drawn together with a passion that took both of us by surprise. I quickly moved some of my things into his townhouse, and we spent a lot of time together. As we talked about our goals and dreams, we discovered that we shared the desire to be married and have children. We made love beautifully, and we liked being together. The fit was very good. After a relatively short time together, Richard proposed marriage. I accepted, thrilled that a smart, successful, handsome man, who wanted a family as much as I did, wanted to marry me. Even though we hadn't yet set a date, I felt that my prayers were being answered.

And yet, amidst the beauty of our connection, amidst the promise of my life dreams being realized, I was plagued by doubts and uncertainties. This was disappointing. I had believed that a committed relationship would heal all ills, and harmony would prevail. I was wrong. Instead of bringing more peace, the presence of a man in my life seemed to trigger my anxiety. I always had trouble trusting men, and the promise of Richard's permanent role in my life brought that to the forefront.

Although Richard and I shared our life's work, although we spoke the same language and were able to communicate in words and ideas that were familiar, there was one area of disconnection. He seemed disdainful of my spiritual quest, and his disdain showed up in subtle ways. Whenever I spoke about my ceremonies and shamanic practices, he became distracted and uninterested. Whenever I pressed him to talk about it, he spoke in disapproving terms. I could discuss ideas about growth with him, but he was limited as to how far he would go with it and what he would accept. I began to feel stilted, but I didn't want to admit it. I was afraid that if I left Richard, I would never find another man who shared common interests with me. It had been a long time since I had met anyone I wanted to date, let alone consider marrying. I wanted a committed relationship very much, but at some level I felt trapped. At first I thought that if I focused on what was good about the relationship, the rest would go away or dissolve into the ethers. It worked for a while, but it was inevitable that my doubts and fears would reappear.

One morning, a few days before Christmas, I was on my way to the gym, sitting in bumper-to-bumper traffic in rush hour, agitated and wishing I were anywhere else. Suddenly, my car started pitching over to one side. I made it through the heavy traffic, pulled over to the shoulder of the freeway, and after a quick inspection, I found a flat right rear tire.

"Damn, what bad timing!" I moaned, trembling both from the cold spell we were having and my frustration about the car. In a matter of minutes, however, a highway patrolman stopped and called the auto club. The freeway was so plugged up, it was a full hour before the truck arrived. By the time the tire was changed, I had missed my workout, so I headed straight home.

I picked up the phone and called Richard to tell him my tale of woe. "I'm so upset," I said. "Two days ago my car battery went dead, I just got over that virus, I got freezing cold on the freeway, and I missed my workout. I'm so stressed out."

Richard's voice, calm and distant across the phone wires, was unsettling. "I understand, but don't go driving around on that skinny spare tire. Go out right away and get a new one," he ordered.

"I'll think about it," I said, irritated by his telling me how to deal with my crisis. I even knew he was right, but I was more interested in an offer to come and help instead of advice. This was just one more thing to do during the busiest time of the year. I shuffled into the kitchen to get a snack, and then I wandered around the living room, munching on a bran muffin, trying to organize the rest of the day. I was just beginning to calm down when I heard a sharp cracking noise followed by a strange hiss. What was that? I walked back into the kitchen and then into the bedroom, trying to figure out what had caused the noises when the fire alarm in the living room went off. I raced into the room just in time to see water pouring through the alarm mechanism. It was running down the walls and the windows, thoroughly soaking the wall-to-wall carpeting. It took me a moment to realize that the pipes in the building had burst and my apartment was flooding. I rushed downstairs to alert the manager, who turned off the water.

I canceled a lunch appointment with a friend, took a deep breath, and went out to buy a new tire. The next day the manager of my building called me at Richard's to tell me that the pipes had burst again. This time the water had run right through the living room, outside the doors, and was dripping off the second-story balcony. Richard drove me home so I could pick up some clothes, and we video-taped the damages for an insurance claim. With each step across the saturated floor, my shoes squeaked and sprayed water. It was a real mess. Then, to add insult to injury, an outside water pipe burst at Richard's house. We spent the rest of the afternoon capping the pipe, certain that there must have been some sort of conspiracy going on.

Exhausted by so many disasters on top of one another, we decided to try distracting ourselves with a movie. It helped. We saw a comedy and laughed a lot. We sat up wrapping Christmas presents, feeling pretty good, until eleven o'clock that night, when the phone rang. We were almost afraid to answer it, but what else could possibly happen? It was Richard's answering service informing him that a water pipe at his office had burst and water was running out the front door and down the street. At midnight, we found ourselves shell-shocked, driving to the office to turn off the water.

I couldn't believe that water pipes in three different locations could have burst within the same two days right before Christmas. What did it mean? It seemed as if my life was in shambles. I couldn't make sense out of so many similar disasters happening at the same time, so I stopped trying. There were other more important things to focus on. Richard and I spent Christmas Eve day cleaning up his office. I was anxious all afternoon, afraid that Richard would get so caught up in the cleanup that he would bow out of my annual family celebration. This was upsetting to consider; I really wanted him with me.

There were two kinds of holiday celebrations in my family. One was on Christmas Eve, which we spent in a wild frenzy munching pizza and opening presents. The other was on Christmas Day, when the family shared a quiet dinner of turkey and the trimmings, sitting around the table for hours eating and visiting. I cherished the quiet time, while I dreaded the night before. My family members, who generally leaned toward the quiet side, chose a few occasions during the year to make a big hoopla. Christmas Eve was one of those times.

Each Christmas Eve, try as I might to become involved in the required merriment and rituals, my eyes would gloss over, and I'd have a hard time following the line of conversation. I felt weighted down by my sense of obligation to join in the appropriate chatter. It was never my nature to chitchat, and I was afraid that in trying, I sounded blunt or out of touch.

My family members would all be dressed impeccably, and Phyllis, my stepmother, would hurry around the living room, making sure everyone had their gifts. The 150-pound mastiff family dog would wade through the debris of ribbon and flying paper wrappings, sniffing out any forgotten or spilled snacks and drooling across shoulders and laps, while Phyllis tossed tea towels to the chosen people to wipe off the slobber. My father, who caught most of the drool, would complain that he had just gotten his slacks back from the cleaners. What inevitably happened was that the noise of the group would overwhelm me, the sudden flashbulbs from Polaroid cameras would blind me, and my stab at enthusiasm would quickly be replaced by a headachy, leaden feeling.

I stood out because I had no mate, and my involvement in a spiritual path seemed to confuse my family, isolating me further. There were other differences: I dressed for comfort; they dressed for glamour. I rarely wore makeup, and to them, my conversation was "heavy." In fact, to them, that's how I made my living: by talking about "heavy" things. They all wanted the mood and the conversation to be light, and the weight of these expectations for lightness produced the opposite effect in me.

Christmas was a time of unexpressed longing in my life, both emotional and spiritual. Alcohol, food, movies, and chatter did nothing to fill the gap. They only made it worse. Standing among my family, all of whom I loved dearly and who meant well and were determined to be happy and festive, made me feel like a square peg trying to fit into a round hole.

This year I had hoped that Christmas Eve would be different. I would be with Richard, and for the first time in years, I would not be the only adult who had no partner. Whether or not I actually felt I fit in, at least I would have someone to go home with and discuss the evening.

I looked around the office. It was a soaking mess; I knew there was no way Richard would leave. My neat little dream was shattered as he told me that he had to stay and finish cleaning up. I was visibly anxious, and he attempted to make me feel better by saying he'd try to come by later.

He never called, and he never came by. I passed the dreaded evening as serenely as I could. I could feel them all watching me, and I imagined them thinking, "Poor Jennifer, that Richard doesn't care enough about her to show up." By the end of the evening, as I sat with cardboard pizza sitting like lead in my stomach, as I watched a lighthearted video with a happy ending, I was sick with disappointment. I could see my hands trembling from fatigue while my stomach hurt and my head throbbed.

It was finally time to leave. My apartment, although still somewhat soggy, was only ten minutes away, and I was afraid that if I saw Richard, I'd let him have it for not calling. I decided I would just go home. I couldn't face a confrontation on Christmas Eve. I needed to lie down and sleep. I knew I'd feel differently in the morning, so I called Richard's office. There was no answer, so I tried his apartment. He picked up the phone.

"Hi, Richard," I said.

"Hi. I just got home. Where are you?" he asked.

"I'm still at the party. I'm exhausted, and I'm going home to sleep. How about if we talk first thing in the morning?"

"In the morning?" he yelled into my ear. "How could you consider not waking up with me on Christmas morning? How can you be so selfish?"

I was shocked at his response. "But you told me that holidays weren't important to you. Is this one different?" My cheeks flushed red. Now I was angry. "And if Christmas is so damned important to you, why didn't you even bother calling me here to say you wouldn't be showing up?"

"Look, Jennifer. I've been working very hard, and I can't handle this emotional display. Just do whatever you want!" He hung up. My anger fell away as quickly as it had come. I dropped the phone back in the cradle and felt my eyes stinging. Phyllis came over as I was trying to hold back my tears.

"What's wrong, honey?" she asked, full of concern. "Are you sure you should be driving? Why don't you stay here with us?"

In the midst of my turmoil, that was the last thing I wanted to do. I assured her I'd be fine, and I left. When I got home, I collapsed on the bed. It seemed like everything in my life was collapsing. My apartment was a wreck, and now my relationship was falling apart. What was happening to me? I dropped off to sleep feeling insecure and frightened, hoping that with a new day, everything would be all right again.

I was awakened early by a phone call. It was Richard. He wanted to talk. He drove right over, and I could tell as soon as he entered the room that he was not in a good mood. He told me how wrong I had been, how insensitive I was to his problems. He felt he had been mistreated and neglected while he went through the stress of cleaning up his office. He refused to have a two-way discussion. In fact, he seemed to feel that I didn't deserve to have a point of view. I felt so confused and guilty by the time he left, I was starting to agree with him. It was a difficult and empty Christmas.

The next day, I found all the presents I had given him in a pile in my office. It was over. We didn't speak for several days. I spent my time putting my apartment back together, replacing the carpet, drying out clothing and furniture upholstery, and trying to exorcise the nauseating stench of mildew that seeped out of the floorboards. I burned incense to get rid of the rotten smell and to purify my home. I felt as if the spiritual currents that I had been building in my home were out of whack, so I burned sage and prayed, trying to reset the energy.

I reorganized my home in the midst of my devastation over what had happened with Richard. At times I felt cruelly abandoned, and the grief was overwhelming.

Often I was panicked and anxious; I couldn't believe what had happened to us. And then, to my surprise, from time to time a sense of calm came over me. I would feel peaceful and quiet inside for a few minutes before the anxiety flooded back in, leaving me shaken and confused. I never knew how I would feel from one moment to the next. I was certainly upset about breaking up with Richard, but it was so much more. I didn't understand that this roller coaster of emotions was not only about my present disappointment; it was also being driven by a lifetime of unmet dependency needs. I attached the full range of emotions to Richard and, soon, all I could think about was finding a way to get him back.

Five days after our fight, I went into the office on a Saturday afternoon to do some paperwork and prepare for the coming week. Richard didn't work on Saturdays, and it seemed like a safe time to focus on myself. Twenty minutes into my work, I looked out the window to see Richard's car pulling into the parking lot. I froze. I had been so sure he wouldn't show up, I hadn't showered, my hair was dirty, and I was wearing my raggiest clothes. "Oh God," I thought. "Please don't let him see me like this." The inevitable knock sounded on the door.

"Come in," I called out.

He walked into the room and stood there like a statue, well-groomed as always, calm, and completely sure of himself. "Jennifer," he said, "you seemed very upset this week. I just wondered if you wanted to talk."

I was stunned into silence for a moment. His eyes were

cold, and he appeared almost disinterested, but he had offered to talk, all by himself. I agreed, as long as we could go into his office, which was larger than mine and less intimate. I felt safer there.

As usual, he spoke first. "Really, Jennifer, I couldn't believe you got angry at me when I was the one who had the bad deal. I had to work in my office on Christmas Eve without your help while you got to spend an enjoyable evening with your family."

I was speechless. I had told him how difficult those evenings were. He had nodded and said all the right things in all the right places. I thought he had understood; in fact, I had taken comfort from that, but apparently he had never heard a word I said. I let him continue his one-way conversation.

"I'm the one who suffered here," he said. "I worked until I was bone weary on Christmas Eve, and I never complained. Your anger was completely absurd and unreasonable. Wouldn't you agree?"

The more he spoke, the less I was able to hold onto my point of view. I hardly knew what to say, but I had to say something. I didn't want to blow this opportunity to work things out. "I understand," I told him. "From your perspective, I see how you felt, and I can accept your feelings. Can you accept mine?"

"No," he said adamantly. "I can't. You're being unreasonable. Can't you see that?"

I burst into tears. All I wanted was some comfort for both of us. I wanted to support him, but I also wanted him to see my side. Richard came over and put his arms around me. "I want a committed relationship with you, and I want to start a family," he announced. It came from out of the blue; I couldn't have been more shocked. Those were the words I was craving to hear, and as soon as he said them, I dropped needing to be heard or understood. I just wanted the relationship back, and I was willing to give up everything else to get what I wanted. The wounded part of me, which had felt abandoned and terrified, relaxed. Maybe he was right after all. Even if he wasn't, I vowed to be more considerate in the future. If I could have him and the family that I wanted, wouldn't it all be worth it?

I melted into his arms, relieved and at the same time fearful. I knew that I was overlooking something, but my need to be accepted overrode all the rest of it. I told myself that a relationship always involved sacrifice and when Richard and I were "on," it felt so right. I would use our disagreement to deepen my commitment. I hoped that the things he had said and his unwillingness to understand me were not a harbinger of similar things to come.

# 7

# MISADVENTURES IN L.A.

IN JANUARY, I HAD SCHEDULED AN APPOINTMENT with Lynn, and I invited Richard to drive with me to Los Angeles. Our life had settled into a better place; it wasn't stress free, but making it through the difficulties over the holidays had brought us closer together. We shared a kind of quiet excitement, and I hoped that our psychological connection might sustain us.

When Richard agreed to accompany me to L.A., I was pleased, but I had a few reservations. I usually stayed at the Beverly Hills Hotel when I went for my sessions. I loved the luxury of it, but I wasn't sure if that would suit Richard. His tastes were more spartan than mine. I suggested to him that perhaps we might stay somewhere less grand and less expensive where he would feel more at home.

"I think the Beverly Hills Hotel will be just fine," he said. "If we split the costs, I don't think it'll be too much."

I was pleased. He was acting amiable, and it seemed as if he wanted to make me happy. Feeling optimistic about the weekend, I made the reservation.

The drive down was great fun. We talked and talked;

this was where Richard and I really connected. When we were in harmony, I got so high from our conversations, I knew that we were meant to be together. We stopped for a leisurely lunch along the way, enjoying just being together. Our ease continued until we were making our approach into the city, when Richard went quiet. I noticed that he seemed to be getting moody and dark.

"Is something wrong?" I asked him.

"No," he said with a slight annoyance in his voice. "I'm just tired."

He didn't speak when we got off the freeway, and I was afraid to try to bring him out. I felt anxious, yearning to return to the lighthearted conversation of the earlier part of the day, and I hoped he would come out of his withdrawal.

It was twilight as we rolled down Sunset Boulevard and turned left up the long driveway that led to the Beverly Hills Hotel. I took a deep breath of relief. The sprawling grounds were beautiful as always, and seeing the greenery helped me to relax. But it seemed to have exactly the opposite effect on Richard. When the doorman opened the door to let him out of the car, Richard's body went completely rigid. We checked into our room, which was wallpapered in pastels and flowers, and Richard immediately started in.

"God, this room feels stuffy. And the walls are ridiculous. How corny can you get!"

"Richard, I don't think it's the room or the walls," I told him. "You've been moody for the last hour. Why don't you tell me what's really going on?"

"It's this place, Jennifer. Can't you feel it? The pretension makes my skin crawl. I can't understand why you like being here."

I had an urge to defend my choice of hotels, to tell him that he had agreed to stay here with me and to enjoy it, but I knew that would be useless. He had made up his mind and, as usual, that was that. He spoke again, this time a little less angry. "Look, I'm just hungry. Let's go get some dinner."

"We could eat here," I suggested, tired from the long drive and not so anxious to get back into the car.

Richard jumped to his feet. "No!" He tossed the room service menu on the floor. "I'm not eating in this place and paying these prices! We're going out."

"All right then, let's go," I said. The irritation was coming through my voice, but I tried to temper it, not wanting to make things any worse than they already were.

We drove into Beverly Hills, and when we got to Rodeo Drive, we found several different restaurants in a row. They were all crowded as it was Saturday night at dinnertime, and after we chose the one that Richard found the least disagreeable, we gave them our names. While we waited, Richard complained about what he called "the Los Angeles dinner crowd." He said they were all self-absorbed and overly concerned about the impression they were making on one another. I found myself wishing Richard were more concerned about the impression he was making on me. When our orders came, he hated his food. He pronounced it inedible and complained bitterly about paying "a fortune" for food he couldn't possibly eat. He insisted that we get up and leave before I was finished.

Once we were back at the hotel, things didn't get any better. His agitation increased as he paced back and forth, muttering to himself. I was angry at this point. I had invited him to spend a special time with me, and all he could do was complain. Determined not to allow his mood to ruin mine any longer, I decided to take care of myself. I took out a book and started to read, completely ignoring him. That was the last straw. He started to cry. I think his tears surprised both of us, and as I put down my book, I wondered if my scheduled session in the morning with Lynn was affecting him. Perhaps some unresolved pain was being unlocked, and this was a cleansing opportunity for Richard. I tried to be compassionate, doing what I could to comfort him. But everything I said seemed to simultaneously comfort and upset him. He alternated between tears and anger. I was completely baffled and afraid I'd be tired for my appointment in the morning, which was the purpose for the trip in the first place.

"Richard, I don't know what to do for you," I said, exasperated. "I came here to do my session with Lynn tomorrow, and I'm completely wiped out. I'm starting to get angry, and I need you to stop and think about me for a change."

He began yelling. "I can't believe how selfish you are! I drive all the way down here, I'm going through something, and all you can think about is yourself. Can't you see I'm having a breakdown, or is Lynn more significant to you than your fiancé? I should be more important than some stupid appointment you can reschedule."

I felt embarrassed. Maybe I was wrong. I had thought he was being selfish, but I wasn't sure anymore. Here it was again: the same confusion I always felt when Richard accused me of selfishness. I quieted down and let him ramble on as he gave me his laundry list of what was wrong with me. I held him while he cried. I rubbed his back and soothed him. He allowed himself to be comforted, but his rage remained just beneath the surface, threatening to resurface if I made the slightest wrong move. The pressure was immense and finally, at 4:00 A.M., his exhaustion got the better of him and we both dropped off to sleep.

I awakened a few hours later and canceled my appointment. I was in no shape to see Lynn. Richard remained upset, coercing me to admit that I had been self-centered and uncaring once again in his hour of greatest need. With almost no sleep and under a relentless onslaught of criticism, I got behind the wheel and we headed back up north.

The further away from Los Angeles we got, the more Richard's mood began to even out. After an hour or two, he actually became somewhat pleasant, his voice softened, and he began to smile. I drove on, still in shock from the night before, but relieved that he was calming down. I was mortified that I had missed my session with Lynn, but it seemed as if I had had no choice. I felt torn apart, as if I

had to decide between my commitment to my relationship and my commitment to the shamanic path. The bat-
tle felt like a physical pain wrenching through my body. It
hurt so badly, I numbed it out and put up my defenses. In
my inability to express my pain, I internalized it, convinc-
ing myself that there were many paths to enlightenment.
Perhaps this whole incident was a sign that I needed to
look into other avenues for spiritual development that
would be more complementary to my relationship.

We didn't speak about what happened for two whole
days, and then when we did, we had another fight. The
mere mention of the weekend exploded into a polariza-
tion. We just couldn't agree about what had happened,
about who was right and who was wrong. Richard would
not budge from his position that I had treated him badly.

"But I stayed up all night long comforting you," I
argued. "How can you say I was selfish?"

"Why do you think it took me so long to calm down?
You tried to comfort me, but your heart wasn't in it.
I'm too perceptive to buy that one. I knew you were
more concerned about your appointment with Lynn
than with me."

Richard was right. I had been quite concerned with
my session. "Yes, I was upset about my work with Lynn,
but I still came from a loving place with you. I can care
about myself and you at the same time. They don't have
to be mutually exclusive, you know."

Richard crossed his arms. "Jennifer, say whatever
you want. Your selfishness during my breakdown was
unpardonable."

We went round and round until finally we decided to separate for a couple of days to think about it. A detached part of me could understand Richard's point of view. He had needed my full attention in a way that I was not available to give. Becoming more loving and present was a direction and a commitment I had chosen for myself. But I also could see validity in my side of the story. Beneath it all, my fear of abandonment, the possibility of the loss of the relationship I wanted so badly, was blinding me to my own needs.

I decided I would use the incident in the hotel room as an opportunity for growth. In the future, I would not ignore my needs, but I would deal with them internally and not expect Richard to participate. It would be worth it. After all, there was so much that worked, such as the wonderful drive we had before Richard became moody. What about the stimulating conversations, the hikes we both enjoyed so much, the goals we shared for raising children? Why couldn't I focus on what worked? Richard was a good provider, and there was an undeniable excitement and psychological understanding between us. If I could find a way to stay composed and bring a loving presence and maturity to our relationship, it couldn't help but work out. Then I'd get all the things that were important to me, and I'd surely become a better person. Wouldn't I? I was so terrified of the alternative, it seemed worth a try.

# 8

# AROUND THE MEDICINE WHEEL

ONE MORE TIME, RICHARD AND I DECIDED THAT we were willing to move forward. My commitment to do what was necessary worked to a certain extent; we had our moments of fun and connection, but they seemed to come around less and less. Richard's disdain of my spiritual quest continued to show up. When I told my best friend, Bonnie, about my feelings, she was concerned.

"I'm worried about you, Jennifer," she said. "You seem to be getting further and further away from what's always been most important in your life. I wish you had stayed in Los Angeles and gone to see Lynn. I think she would've had some good insights for you about what's going on in your relationship."

I nodded and shrugged. I wasn't exactly sure if I had even wanted Lynn's input. I was more afraid of it than anything else. What if she told me to leave Richard? What if she didn't approve of us being together? What would happen to my dreams?

Bonnie went on. "You hardly laugh anymore. Did you know that?"

71

"Yes, I know." I had to agree with her. I was less spontaneous and cheerful recently. Life felt as if I were wading through something thick and sticky. "I know he's heavy, but I'm sure it's just a phase," I rationalized to my friend. "I've had a lot of shamanic training. I can handle this cycle with maturity and wisdom. What have I been learning all this for if I can't use it to improve my life?"

Bonnie looked skeptical. I laughed. "Maybe I'll become a Buddhist," I said. "Then I can just meditate myself into oblivion."

"Listen, Jennifer, I know how much you want a baby and a husband. But I can't stand watching you giving yourself up to fit into a mold Richard's creating for you."

I decided to call Lynn. Maybe she could help me. I was ready to take responsibility for my uncomfortable feelings, and I wanted to learn to be a better partner and mate. I wasn't able to make the trip to Los Angeles at this time, but Lynn didn't mind. She agreed to do a telephone session with me.

"What do you want?" she asked, her tone warm and attentive. She always came straight to the point.

"I want to be more yielding in my relationship," I said.

"All right. Are you somewhere you can lie down?"

"Yes."

"Good. Close your eyes. I want you to go inside and create a medicine wheel. See yourself in a protected spot in the wilderness, someplace very beautiful. Now gather the different rocks to represent each of the four directions the way I've taught you. Begin at the south, then move clockwise to the west, over to the north, and finish with the east. Say a prayer to each direction as you place the rocks. Take your time. I'll wait, and you let me know when you're finished."

I did as she directed me. I knew that it didn't matter that we were on the phone. To Lynn and her medicine teachers, the sacredness of the medicine circle, whether it was in a physical manifestation or in my mind's eye, was the same. It still represented balance and wholeness.

I traveled in my mind. I imagined a round, balanced rock for the south. When Lynn first taught me about the south, she had instructed me, "Live within the lodge of your innocence." She told me that maintaining innocence was listening to my own inner voice, knowing that the powers of the universe are within each of us. Nurturing, virtue, balance, flow, and skills that offer quickening and commitment are qualities associated with the south.

When I pictured my dark rock for the west, I thought about introspection, mystery, and the transformation that comes with grief. "A shaman can teach you about power," Lynn had written in *The Power Deck* (New York: Harper-Collins, 1991, p. 61). "A magician can train you to become strong in spirit and competent in your endeavors in life. But to describe how a miracle happens or how you become a powerful magician is to try to explain the mystery. You can talk around the secrets of power, but if you describe them directly, you lose that power and you destroy the mystery. Welcome it, and allow the miracle of existence to emerge from the darkness and transform you."

I created a strong rock for the north, a place of gathering and centering. In *The Power Deck* (p. 79), Lynn had described gathering like this: "This life is like a fulcrum on a scale of balance. Your past and future lives determine the need for gathering strength in this life. There is a reason for all the pain. As you gather knowledge from the infinite sea of consciousness and life experience, you may begin to evolve. . . . Become one with all life, and consider the true importance of what you are gathering."

Finally, I chose a sparkling golden rock for the east. In *The Power Deck* (p. 103), Lynn had written about illumination: "As darkness comes, the mirrors of your spirit reflect different images. . . . Reflect on the new vision that has been living on the perimeter of your consciousness. . . . The totality of your creativity comes after you have begun your work on the sacred painting of your life. . . . Take responsibility for your work and your life, and then illumination will follow."

I looked around my medicine wheel, satisfied with the wholeness, with the possibilities it suggested for who I truly was and for reality itself. As I breathed in the energies of the four directions and offered up my prayers, I got in touch with a sense of my totality. I saw the wheel as a mirror for my strengths and my weaknesses. It all felt right.

"I'm ready," I said.

Lynn continued her directions. "I want you to place a red blanket in the center of the wheel and set your sacred objects on it. Sit on the blanket facing the south. See the little girl who lives inside you sitting in the south."

"I can see her," I whispered.

"Ask your little girl how she feels about your relationship with Richard."

"She's a little shaky about it. She likes the physical stuff, the playing and wrestling, but she doesn't like it when he criticizes her."

"Now ask her how she thinks Richard's little boy likes her."

I smiled. "She knows he likes her a lot."

"Thank her for talking to us. Now change directions. Move to the west on the wheel, and let's dialogue with your teenager. How does she feel about Richard?"

"She thinks he's sexy, but she fights with him a lot. She gets contrary and likes to argue."

"How does Richard feel about her?"

"He thinks she's sexy, too, but he argues with her, and he just won't give in. He really believes he's right." I paused a minute, taking in the information, grateful to understand which parts of me were creating my difficulties.

Lynn called me back to the present. "Jennifer, thank your teenager, and let's move to the north. This is the inner adult. What does she have to tell you?"

"She doesn't have a problem with Richard, but she has a hard time comforting the little girl. When Richard hurts her feelings, the little one becomes inconsolable and that's where the real work is."

"How does Richard's adult feel about her?"

"He feels fine about her. I don't pick up anything unusual or overly emotional toward her."

"Okay. Time to move to the east. Ask the Wise One how she feels about your relationship."

I felt as though I were facing a sacred being inside of me, and I was filled with a deep reverence. "She finds the whole thing full of humor. She's delighted with all of it, especially the struggles. I guess she sees the growth potential in it."

Lynn allowed me to silently acknowledge the Wise One, and then we were back in the present moment. I opened my eyes.

"How do you feel about the ceremony?" Lynn wanted to know.

"I feel good about it. I feel calmer about the difficult parts. I see that I need to mediate my teenager so there's less conflict. That's really where it's all coming from."

"I know you can do it. Seeing it and understanding is a fine beginning." Lynn went on to describe some additional ceremonial tasks that she thought would be helpful.

"It's time to make your grief doll," she told me.

I felt instant irritation. Making dolls was an integral part of my work with Lynn, one that I had looked forward to in the past. Each year I participated in group work with Lynn where we gathered sacred materials and objects and created two dolls that represented specific qualities for our work. One doll stood for the particular direction we were working in at the time and was a goddess power doll.

In the south was the conjurer doll; in the west, the transformational doll; in the north, the rainbow doll; and in the east, the heyoka, sacred clown doll. We used organic materials like sunflower seeds or corn or stones and twigs to create parts of the bodies and souls of these dolls. They were to be placed on our personal altars, which in conjunction with our other sacred objects, was a way to choreograph spiritual energy. It was in front of these altars that we would meditate and seek to find answers to our various problems.

In addition to the dolls representing the different qualities of the goddess, others were extensions of our unfinished business. The first year, we made what we called twisted arm dolls to personify our anger. This year, the assignment had been to make a grief doll. We were instructed to make her out of appropriate materials that felt like our grief. Her head represented the Mother; her legs, the Father; the front, our childhood; and the back, our present life. The left arm represented our sisters or other females who had caused us grief in our childhood, and the right arm represented the males who had done the same.

I had resisted making my grief doll. I couldn't see a reason when we got the assignment, and I didn't see a reason now. What was the point anyway? I was trying to find a way to make my relationship work. How could grief from my past have anything to do with Richard?

I hung up the phone feeling burdened, an unusual feeling for me in relation to my medicine work. I almost always embraced this work with enthusiasm. Lynn called it "confronting my self-wound," and I usually loved doing it. But today I felt rebellious. I considered dismissing her suggestion. I was in a major relationship with a man who wanted to marry me. I didn't have the spare time to devote to making dolls.

My mind spun out. What was the point of all this shamanism anyway? I had gotten what I asked for: a good career in the healing arts and a promising relationship with a man who wanted children. Maybe I had arrived. What was the use of continuing on a spiritual path that felt cumbersome and at cross-purposes with what I wanted for myself? Maybe Lynn didn't know what she was talking about. Although she was clearly a woman of great abilities and perceptions, her judgment might be off in this case. Maybe I should be a little bit more wary of her suggestions. I had some thinking to do. My mind swirled around with doubts and questions until well into the middle of the night, when I finally fell into a troubled sleep.

# 9

# COMMITMENT VERSUS TRUTH

KALA CAME TO SEE ME INITIALLY TO WORK ON HER self-esteem. She had been raised in a traditional Chinese family, her parents' high expectations leaving her with feelings of inadequacy. She had a successful career as an engineer, but she always felt like she just didn't measure up. She couldn't derive satisfaction from any of her accomplishments; it was as if she carried a heavy burden on her back at all times. Kala needed to let go of the past, to see who she was today, and to separate her own values from those of her family.

We had worked together for several months when Kala discovered that more than anything, she wanted a relationship. Not a partnership that would please her parents, but an intimate connection with a man that would feed her deeper needs and provide her with the warmth she had never received from her family. She hadn't a clue what that would look like, and as we delved into her confusion, I spoke to her about the importance of the day-to-day aspects of relationships.

"If what you really want is emotional presence and commitment," I told her, "it has to be balanced with the practical needs of surviving in the world together." I wondered if I were talking to Kala or myself. "Why don't you make out a list of all the qualities you want in a man?" I suggested.

We were sitting on the back porch of my office, enjoying the hint of jasmine that rode the air currents, and allowing the sun to warm our faces. "But I'm afraid to talk about them," she told me. "What if they turn out to be unrealistic?"

"If you don't give yourself permission to ask for what you want, how will you recognize a good fit when you see it?"

"You mean it's really okay to ask for what I want?"

I removed my sunglasses and looked Kala straight in the eye. "Yes. The universe needs you to be specific. How else will it know what to manifest for you?"

"I can have whatever I want just by asking?"

I sat back in my chair, searching for a way to allow her to understand me better. "Kala, it doesn't work exactly like that, but it's a good beginning. What you're doing is making yourself receptive. Women need to be able to receive, to hold and contain what we want in life. Even if it's something we don't know about completely."

I remembered Agnes's words to Lynn: "Ripen your receptive void like a womb accepting a seed. Open yourself to the unknowable so that the energy of what you need can flow into you."

Kala looked thoughtful.

"So tell me what will be different about you when you

have the relationship you're looking for," I said, encouraging her to probe her own mind.

Kala smoothed her shiny dark hair back from her face. "I'll have more confidence in myself. And I'll be more peaceful and centered. I guess I'll just be happier."

"My teacher's guide once told her, 'Identify the form of the power you want, what you want to accomplish, create, or be. Then become it, so that there is no separation between who you are and what you wish to become.' I think what she meant was that in order to find what you're looking for, you have to become it first. Does that make sense to you?"

"I think so." Kala nodded dubiously.

I continued. "I want you to practice being peaceful and centered. Gather your focus and intent. Choose your happiness."

She sat up taller in her chair. "How can I do that?" she demanded, her face flushed, her voice so fierce, it bordered on angry.

My words had challenged her. I needed to meet her intensity. "Kala, you may not want to hear this, but your happiness will never come from outside yourself, not from your family, not from a relationship with a man. The only way to be happy is to find it first in yourself and then bring it to the relationship. Once you're happy inside, you become a magnet."

Kala shook her head. This thinking was obviously turning her own thoughts upside down, and she didn't like it. When Lynn had tried to change my thoughts about this,

I had resisted, too. Even now, I could see Lynn haunting me, the top half of her long blond hair pulled back by a large blue bow, the rest of her hair scattered around her shoulders wild and free, framing her face like a lioness. Her words had pierced my insides. "In order for real change to happen, we have to move out of our entrenched ways of perceiving the world to make room for something new." As I watched Kala struggling to hold onto the past, I understood her difficulty. I still hadn't fully made the change in myself, judging by my continuing battles with Richard. I wondered if Kala would be more successful than I, or if we would both continue to struggle.

One afternoon at our regular appointment time, Kala burst into my office, shivering with excitement. "It's *him*! I've met him!" she exploded. Her face was rosy, and a strange humming sound seemed to be emanating from her.

I wanted to join in her enthusiasm, but something told me to hold back. "That's great." I responded with coolness. "Tell me more."

"I was at the market when I ran into a friend who was having a barbecue that evening. She invited me to come. At first I wasn't sure if I should go, but then I remembered you saying that I needed to be more open, so I said yes. I was sitting there having a beer when he walked in. He came right up to me, Jennifer, and we started talking. His name is Joel. We talked all night long. I felt really close to him; it was like putting on an old sweater. He said he'd call the next day, but the only thing that bothered me was that he waited three days to call. Do you think that's a problem? But he called. He said he'd call again the next day, but that was two days ago. What do you think?" She was almost panting.

I felt reserved. "It sounds like you two hit it off. What do you like about him?"

"He's totally honest. He's having trouble at work—he owns a construction firm and it's slow—but he's dedicated to making it work. He wasn't afraid to tell me that things weren't going well. I think that takes courage, don't you? He has an eight-year-old daughter, and he and his ex-wife split up when his daughter was very small. He wants more kids, and so do I. He's so cute."

Information spilled out of Kala like dammed waters being let loose. I listened, unable to catch her excitement. "This is wonderful news," I said. "So tell me more."

I remembered a conversation I had had with Lynn about Richard. I was singing his praises to her, leaving out the problems. I hadn't been convinced myself, and I wanted her to reassure me that everything was all right. But she hadn't. She had just kept saying, "That's great, honey. Tell me more." I looked at Kala, a larger than life reflection of myself. All I could see was her desperation, her need to be assured. And in good conscience, I couldn't do it. In that moment, I was scared for both of us.

"There is one strange thing," Kala said in a quiet voice. She paused, reluctant to continue.

"What is it?" I asked gently.

"Well, it's really nothing, but for the past several months, Joel's ex-wife, Sally, has been living with him. He says it's temporary, but he thinks it's good for his daughter to have them all living together. You know, family and everything."

"What?" The reaction burst out of my mouth before I had a chance to think about it.

Kala rushed in. "No, no. It's not what you think. They're not together. He's going to build her a cottage on his property so their daughter can go back and forth between them more easily. After all, she's only eight. Did I already tell you that?" Kala was breathless.

I regained my composure. "And this seems reasonable to you?"

Kala shook her head no and at the same time said, "Yes. Maybe something like that could be nice, like a community or something. I met her and her parents at the party, and they were all very nice to me. In fact, Sally's parents invited me to a family gathering they're having next week. Isn't that nice of them? Well, I'm sure Joel had something to do with the invitation, but, still, they're so friendly. So is Sally."

"People who get divorced usually don't live together. If they're still living together, why did they get divorced? Something seems very wrong here, and I hope you'll pay attention. I think you need to find out more about this."

Kala looked distraught. "Really, Jennifer, if you could hear Joel explain it, you'd understand. He's completely honest, and he says it's okay."

I shrugged my shoulders. I did understand, better than

she knew. And now I was asking her to do something I hadn't had the courage to do for myself. I knew it was doubtful she'd go for it, but I had to pass on the wisdom regardless of my own strengths and weaknesses. "Why don't you test the relationship?" I suggested, just as Lynn had once told me to do. "You know that any new relationship needs testing to tell you whether it really fits. If it's right, it'll pass the test with flying colors. If it isn't, you should know now."

Kala laughed nervously. "No, no, no. Jennifer, he's so nice. Joel is everything on my list. Really." Who was she trying to convince with the pleading quality in her voice?

I was persistent. "Something isn't right here, and you need to pay attention. The part about his ex-wife living with him does not make sense. I don't know what's going on, but something's off. Be aware, and observe the whole thing carefully. I know you've been lonely, and I don't want you to get hurt."

She nodded her head and, without another word, left. I felt pain in my heart. I wasn't sure if I had been too persistent, but I had to follow my feelings. Saying a brief prayer for Kala and for spirit to guide me in my work, I let it go, knowing that only time could determine the outcome.

Kala canceled her sessions for the next several weeks. I was sorry but not surprised. I was the fly in the ointment, an influence that would not support her blindness. If she wanted to stay in denial, she would have to get away from me. Then one evening she called, asking for an emergency appointment. I set it up for the next day. When she walked in the door, I was startled by her appearance. Normally an impeccable dresser, Kala looked like a mess; her hair was disheveled, she was wearing torn sweatpants and an oversized shirt with a chocolate stain on the front. She sat down, twisting her hands together, avoiding my eyes.

"Joel is still married," she said. "I found out two days ago. We were talking about moving in together and sharing a life, and now I find out he's married!"

"How did you find out?"

"I was out of town on a business trip. I called to check in, to tell him how much I missed him, and when he wasn't home, I called his office. They said he was away. I got this flash—I knew he was with her—so I did a terrible thing." She hesitated, looking at me to see if I was judging her. I nodded encouragement, and she went on. "I knew where Sally worked—she had told me—so I called her office. Her voice mail said she was on vacation. I knew they were together, so when Joel got back, I confronted him."

Kala was ragged with emotion, her hands were shaking, and her lips were trembling with rage. I spoke to calm her and to help her continue talking. "That was very smart of you to follow up on your hunch. What did he say when you confronted him?"

"You won't believe it. He told me that they did go out of town together and that they were still married, but there was nothing for me to be concerned about. He never even apologized for lying. He just said that Sally knew their time together was coming to an end and that nothing sexual had happened, so I had nothing to be upset about."

"How did you feel when he told you?"

"Awful. He lied to me. But you haven't heard the worst of it. He told me he was hurt that I had doubted him and his feelings for me. Can you imagine?"

Yes, I could imagine. She was looking straight at me now. "The scariest part is how much I wanted to believe him and make it all okay. I actually heard myself apologizing for questioning him. That was when I realized something was wrong, and I heard your warning. I told him since he was living with her, eating with her, taking vacations with her, and still married, he had no room for me in his life."

"I'm proud of you, Kala. You created clarity about what you wanted. Maybe this was a test to see if you would settle, or if you really meant what you said. You passed."

Kala left, saddened by the circumstances, but stronger within herself. I knew that it was only a matter of time until she found what she was looking for. As I sat in meditation that evening, I heard Agnes's words to Lynn, "Power will always test you to see if you are worthy. So when you say you want something, power will put roadblocks in your way to see if you are strong enough to surmount them. It is the way of power."

I dropped off to sleep on the trail of these wise words, wondering if it always worked that way, afraid for my own situation. I obviously still had some work to do.

# 10

## THE ECLIPSE

RICHARD AND I HAD SOMEHOW MANAGED TO MAINTAIN a steady degree of harmony over several weeks, and I was encouraged. Maybe we had gotten through the worst of it and all was well. I didn't choose to recognize that my efforts so greatly overshadowed his. All I knew was that things were better, and I held onto a shred of hope that we would work it out.

One afternoon while Richard was planning a business retreat to a beautiful sanctuary in Monterey called Asilomar, he turned to me unexpectedly and said, "While I'm away, why don't you pick out a wedding date?"

I looked at him with amazement. "It means so much to me that you would let me choose the date. It lets me know that you trust me," I told him, overwhelmed with joy and relief. I began to cry.

He reached over and squeezed my hand. "Of course I trust you and I love you. We can marry whenever you say."

I called Bonnie to tell her the news. She exploded at me. "Are you nuts? You told me that you were going to test the relationship for a while to see if Richard is capable of doing anything for you just because it makes you happy, regardless of whether or not he wants to do it. Have you tested him yet? What has he done? Has anything changed?" Her voice was harsh and exasperated.

"I know. I know what I said," I replied, obviously avoiding her questions. "But now everything is different. I'm getting married. And I want you to help me plan the wedding and be my witness. You're my best friend, aren't you?"

"Okay, Jennifer, but I hope you know what you're doing."

Richard and I were married in a small ceremony by his best friend Sam, who was a fellow therapist and an ordained minister. His wife and Bonnie were our witnesses at the wedding. The ceremony was short, and when it was over, the five of us went out to a Chinese restaurant for dinner.

During the course of the meal, Bonnie and Sam's wife talked nonstop. They seemed to have a lot in common, and I felt an old familiar feeling that I was fading away and wasn't there at all. I pushed my chair a little closer to Richard and put my foot next to his, touching him for comfort. He gently moved my foot away and said quietly, "Please don't crowd me, Jennifer." This was not the response I was looking for. I stayed to myself during the rest of the meal. Immediately after dinner, we said good-bye to our guests and everyone went home.

We closed the apartment door behind us, and together

we walked upstairs. We stepped into our bedroom, sat on the bed, looked into each other's eyes, and Richard yawned. "I'm unbelievably tired," he said. "Let's go to bed." He got up, undressed, brushed his teeth, crawled into bed on his side, and promptly fell asleep. I watched him in dismay, still stinging from his retreat in the restaurant. I considered snuggling close to him, but I was afraid of more rejection. This was not how I had pictured my wedding night, but it seemed that nothing was ever the way I pictured it.

I talked silently to myself, trying to make everything okay. "He's probably just weary from the day. I don't need to waste any energy doubting Richard anymore. I can trust in his love now. After all, he married me. What better reassurance could I ask for?" I dropped off to sleep in doubt anyway.

One month after Richard and I were married, I discovered I was pregnant. I was thrilled; this was what I had always wanted. But at the same time, my doubts came pouring in. It was the same dichotomy, the sense of being torn apart that had been present every step of the way in my relationship with Richard.

The blessed news came via a home pregnancy test. When I saw that the results were positive, I rushed in to show Richard. Since his desire for a baby had always equaled mine, I naturally expected him to be as excited as I was.

"That's great, Jen," he said, with a half-smile and a far-off look in his eye. He picked up the newspaper.

"Is that all you're going to say? Aren't you happy?" I tried to press through his silence.

"Yes, of course I'm happy, but you already know that. And you know me. This is just too much for me to take in right now." He went back to his newspaper.

A familiar loneliness hit me in the pit of my stomach. This was Richard. He'd deal with it in his own way in his own time. I remembered my commitment to attend to my feelings by myself. I immediately began to rationalize his behavior, something I had become very good at doing. If Richard was too overwhelmed to react, then I should be grateful for having such a sensitive husband who was so profoundly affected by things. As much as I wanted to share the joy of the moment with him, he obviously needed his private time to take in the enormity of such a miracle. It made sense that it would take him longer to feel it and process it. After all, it was happening in my body, not his.

As much as I could accept this mentally, I still felt disappointed and disconnected. I went within and claimed the experience for myself; there was nothing else I could do. When Richard was able to feel it and share it, I'd be there.

My first weeks of pregnancy coincided with my preparations to attend my yearly conference with Lynn at a metaphysical institute in the high Mojave Desert called Joshua Tree. During my first trimester, I was tired and sick quite a lot. As I packed my bags and thought about the long days and nights of medicine work ahead of me, I wondered how I would ever make the ten-hour trip and participate in the work of a fully packed seminar. Richard couldn't believe I was even considering it. He was a great deal more articulate with his disapproval over my traveling than he had been over my announcement of the pregnancy.

"The first trimester is when most miscarriages happen. Certainly you know this better than I do," he scolded me. "Traveling is dangerous right now, and actually I'm quite surprised at you. I would think you'd make your baby's well-being a first priority in your life and skip this workshop."

Pictures of the ceremonial energy and what would be asked of me gained intensity in my mind until I was overcome with fear, exacerbated by the way my hormones were fluctuating. Richard's condemnation only added fuel to my fear. I imagined having a miscarriage in Joshua Tree and Richard never forgiving me. After a particularly stressful night, wrestling first with insomnia and then with a bout of bad dreams, I decided that Richard was right. I had to make the baby my first priority. I canceled my space at the workshop.

I was relieved that I was taking care of myself, and I felt an instant release of tension. It wasn't until the actual weekend of the workshop that grief overcame me. I woke up on Friday morning knowing that I was missing something irretrievable. I would never be able to recreate the shamanic experience that Lynn and the other women were having. I saw clearly that disconnecting from Lynn was not good for me—not for my growth or for my heart. As a result of the pain I felt by missing the weekend, I embraced shamanism once again with a quickening I could feel in my belly as surely as the life that was growing there.

I saw that Lynn's teachings were more authentic and nourishing than anything else in my life, and I was not willing to give them up. Not for my family, not for Richard, not for a baby, not for anyone. My doubts surrounding Lynn were fully resolved. From now on, Richard would be the one to adjust to his wife's spiritual journey. As I endured the sadness of missing what meant most to me in the world, I restated my commitment. I would continue my work with Lynn no matter what happened. This absolute knowing gave me a kind of peace I had not felt for a long time. I would balance and integrate it all together; the tearing apart was over.

Lynn had instructed me to see the events in my life as a mirror. In this way, the pain of disconnection from my spiritual source became a catalyst to deepen my level of work. To translate my commitment into action, I made an appointment to see Lynn. Unbeknownst to me, I had scheduled my session at the exact moment of an upcoming solar eclipse.

Once at her house, we began our work together with a moment of silence as I went deep inside myself to find images and symbols in my subconscious that were meaningful to me. Suddenly I felt a magical presence in the room. It was almost tangible; I felt that I could reach out and touch a magnetic wave of energy connecting me to Lynn.

"Do you feel it?" she asked, her eyes snapping open.

I nodded.

"Let's go up to the balcony and watch the eclipse together," she said excitedly, like a young child who could hardly restrain herself. We darted up the stairs together, two at a time, and when we reached the upper landing, Lynn handed me a pair of sunglasses. As we passed through her bedroom, I took shy glances at her large bed covered in furs. I had never expected to see her bedroom, and although I didn't want her to think I was snooping, I couldn't help but scan the inner sanctums of my teacher's dreamtime. We walked out onto the stucco balcony that overlooked massive oak trees and brush-covered hills. It was like a private party, just Lynn and me, and I felt honored and excited to be here with her, celebrating a natural magical phenomenon in an intimate setting.

I continued to feel a magnetic current running between us, connecting us one to the other. We lounged on the rattan patio furniture, allowing any free-floating negativity to release into the shadow of the eclipse. Despite the eclipse, the sun seemed unusually bright, intensifying the vivid blue of the sky, contrasting with the greenery growing in splotches against the hillsides. Although the heat felt stifling to me, it didn't seem to disturb a hawk in the sky directly above us, circling lazily on the warm currents of air. I saw Lynn's eyes turn in his direction, acknowledging the sacred messenger of the Great Spirit. We were truly blessed by his presence.

Lynn turned to me, her eyes hidden by the dark glasses. "You are preparing to walk through the gateway of motherhood," she declared. "It's time to leave behind your unresolved childishness. Please lie back."

We both removed our glasses, and I lay back on my lounge chair, breathing in the heat of the day, basking in the energy that linked me with my teacher and to Nature herself. As always, we began in silence, allowing our minds to quiet down and calling in the spiritual energies that lay the foundation for ceremony.

Lynn spoke. "Jennifer, we are going to climb a mountain. Along the way, you will be releasing all that is unresolved within you. By the time we reach the top, you will be a clear vessel. Let's begin right here at the base. What do you need to let go of in your physical body so that you can begin to climb the mountain in front of you?"

I thought for a moment. "My excess weight," I told her. My voice came out as if in a dream.

"Breathe deeply, and see the part of you that represents your excess weight falling away from your body."

With each breath, I saw the heaviness of my body falling down into Mother Earth. Then we began to climb. I felt light as air, heading slowly up the mountainside, devoid of the usual weight of gravity.

"Stop now!" Lynn commanded. "This is a rest point. What do you need to drop in your emotional body to continue the climb?"

"My childishness and fear," I said without hesitation. I breathed deeply as these emotions fell away and drifted down the mountainside to settle into the depths of Mother Earth. I continued to climb.

At the next stop, I released my attachment to intellectualizing and needing to be right. As these mental encumbrances fell away, I felt a lightness in my head. We were now three-quarters of the way up the mountain.

"We're going to stop here for a moment," Lynn told me. "Come with me out onto this ledge. See the openness of the valley below, and tell me about the blocks to your spiritual self that need to be released so we can reach the top of this mountain."

I looked below me. The hillsides and the earth spanned out in such spaciousness, I was in awe of all that Mother Nature was showing me. I saw how powerful she was and how little control there was beyond her bidding. "Control," I said. "I need to let go of the illusion of control." I willingly allowed this last burden to fall away, to drop down the mountain and dissolve into the nothingness from which it had formed. Then I bounded to the top of the mountain, unencumbered, needing nothing, completely connected to all that was around me.

"Visualize the Pleiades constellation. It's a diamond-shaped star system, very sacred to the feminine medicine teachings. Three hundred thousand years ago, the star nations from the Pleiades seeded this planet with great knowledge. The wisdom lies within the trees that you see beneath us, it flows through the vast oceans, it settles in the earth of the tallest mountains. This knowledge has been passed down in the form of medicine teachings through certain women throughout the indigenous cultures of the world."

I was stunned by her words. I had heard her speak of this group of women before, but I never knew who they really were. Now I did. These women were known collectively as the Sisterhood of the Shields, and I understood that Lynn was one of them and that they were all teachers to me. This must have been the inexplicable magnetic energy that I had felt as the eclipse first began, connecting me to Lynn in a way I had never felt before. The flesh on my arms and legs stood out in goosebumps as I realized that one of the Sisterhood of the Shields was actually standing beside me, that I also was connected to them and to the Pleiades.

"As we journey to the Pleiades," Lynn said, "pick one of the stars that you find most attractive and, through it, enter this sacred star system."

I approached the diamondlike configuration and asked Lynn's permission to enter into the center of the system. I could hear the excitement in her voice as she granted me permission. Feeling as light and shimmering as a star, I propelled my weightless dream body through the opening. I floated above a fragrant garden. The brilliance of the colors, the sweetness of the scents, the compelling shapes of the flowers and vegetation that grew here let me know I was standing in the very center of life itself. I breathed it in. I was timeless and a part of the great void, a vessel for the vast knowledge that women have birthed since the beginning of creation. I knew that my pregnancy was a part of this and was being blessed by the goodness and beauty in the world.

I had no idea how much time had passed when we left this alternate reality. I couldn't remember walking back down the stairs when we finally stood in front of Lynn's front door to say good-bye.

"Thanks, Jennifer. I had a good time," Lynn said, hugging me. She had never said that before. "When you are six months along, come back and we'll do some more work, honey."

I walked to my car feeling slightly starry-eyed, grateful that I had not abandoned my shamanic journey.

# 11

## QUICKENING OF THE HEART

AFTER SIX MONTHS OF GROWING INSIDE OF ME, MY unborn child already felt like a being. I named him Gregory. As much as his presence was bringing out my positive mothering qualities, as much as I was committed to my good intentions and my healing path, Gregory also was acting as a dark mirror, reflecting my feelings of deprivation and hopelessness in finding real emotional support. I observed myself carefully during this time, and I was shocked to discover that I had a lot of tension and anger. My pregnancy made me excruciatingly aware of my paranoia and how much I took everything personally. I was ashamed of this bumbling and desperate reflection my son was providing for me, and I was determined to do what I could to heal this aspect of myself.

I did as Lynn suggested: I went back to see her when I was in my sixth month. It wasn't surprising that she started out my session by instructing me to dialogue with Gregory. I had already been doing this on my own, so it seemed natural to continue with Lynn. I knew that my distortions and misinterpretations of the circumstances around me were at the core of my negativity, and I hoped that by confronting them head-on, I could transform them into something that would be positive for Gregory and me.

I had spoken to Gregory in utero many times when we were alone, telling him that these negative thoughts and feelings were mine, not his. I had told him that he didn't need to take them on or even identify with them in any way. "In fact," I had said to him one day, "you never have to take on anybody else's thoughts or feelings." I had hoped that these conversations would serve as a stopgap measure until my session.

Under Lynn's guidance, I continued the discussion. "Tell him about your internal stress," she suggested. "Let him know that you understand his discomfort and you know he doesn't like a stress-filled environment."

I spoke lovingly to my son, and I made an agreement with him that I would do all that I could to heal this pattern in myself. When I agreed to listen well to his feelings of upset, I felt my womb relax. I talked to Gregory about whatever came into my mind, and Lynn listened quietly. The idea of speaking to him was fine—I was accustomed to doing this by myself—but I had a hard time doing it in front of someone else, especially Lynn. I was uncomfortable with her silence, interpreting it as disapproval. I wondered if she found me insincere.

There it was again! Even in Lynn's presence, my suspicions and accusations of myself rolled on unremittingly. They seemed ingrained, woven into the very fabric of my cells. I wanted to weep from my sense of hopelessness about eradicating these dark blotches inside of me. But more than that, I did not want anyone, especially Lynn, to know how personally flawed I felt. I said nothing about this to Lynn, determined to persevere on my own to cleanse and replenish my own soul.

In the last few minutes of our work together, Lynn got a dreamy look in her eye. "Oh, Jennifer," she said, "the baby loves being close to your heart. He delights in your energy. You have such a good heart, honey. I'm not sure he wants to leave. He might want to hold on because he doesn't want to lose that connection with you. If your labor stops midway, be sure and tell him he can have your love on the outside, too."

As she spoke, the darkness flew out of my body like bats winging their way through the air. In Lynn's ability to see beyond my shadow and into my goodness, I felt somehow redeemed. I walked out of there on a cloud. Lynn had said I had a good heart! The voice inside of me that had been denigrating me for so long had just received a large shot of healing energy. I felt my heart solid and powerful, certain in its capacity to love. I could now reclaim a truth about myself. A huge, dense blob of self-doubt crumbled away; I knew that I was truly loved and capable of giving love.

Several days after seeing Lynn, I spoke with Ellen, one of Richard's close friends since his childhood. I was exuberant about being pregnant and about life in general. She was happy for me. "I'm so glad to see you like this and I'm especially happy to see what this is bringing out in

Richard," she said. "I love watching how attentive and tender he is toward you. Too bad it won't last."

"What do you mean?" I asked her, becoming defensive.

"What I mean is that Richard is acting loving because you're pregnant. I know Richard and, believe me, it won't last!"

I decided to pay no attention to this; it was just negativity, the very thought forms that I was fighting so hard to keep away. But her words echoed in my mind. Ellen knew that while Richard appeared mild mannered, he had a great deal of anger beneath the surface. I recalled one particularly disturbing event that had happened when I was four months pregnant.

Richard and I were arguing over which room would be the nursery. When he wouldn't listen to my side of the story, I became agitated. I had begun to walk into the room that I thought more appropriate when he placed his body directly in front of mine, blocking the doorway. Feeling trapped and frightened, I tried to push past him, and in the physical struggle that followed, he hit my upper arm with a closed fist.

Infuriated, I screamed as loudly as I could, "Move aside!"

Richard looked startled and uttered in a maddeningly quiet voice, "I just can't talk to you when you're like this."

He turned and went downstairs. I exhaled and crumbled to the floor. Pain seared through my arm. It had all happened so quickly, I wasn't sure exactly what had occurred. My arm was throbbing, and I noticed a numbness setting in. I remembered a course I had studied on domestic violence in school. They told us that once violence occurs, it continues and escalates over time. I couldn't allow this, not for myself or my baby. I slowly walked downstairs and found Richard sitting in his favorite chair, hiding behind the newspaper.

"Richard, you struck me. I can't have it. I'm leaving this relationship."

Richard let the paper fall quietly into his lap, feigning a shocked facial expression. "Oh, Jennifer. I'm afraid that one of us is very confused about what just happened. This makes me sad."

His tone was soft, his body posture gentle, giving off an unspoken invitation to reconnect. I melted. I became tearful. I so wanted his love and tenderness right now. Maybe I had misinterpreted what happened. Maybe he had hit me inadvertently. He never had been physically violent before. I sank into his lap, and he stroked my hair.

"Okay," I said. "I'll stay. But we have go to couple's therapy."

To my amazement, he agreed. We started soon after that, but neither of us ever mentioned the fight in our sessions. Maybe I was afraid that he would turn it around, that it would all come back on me and would be our final undoing. Whatever the reason, I decided to just leave it alone and made a promise to myself that if it ever happened again, I would take the appropriate steps. In this way I let it go, but things were never quite the same. I was wary in a new way. I watched myself and I watched

Richard carefully, which created a great deal more stress than before. I didn't quite trust him, but I took comfort in the fact that he was willing to go to therapy to work on our relationship. There were a lot of men who would never do that.

Concerning the actual fight, I had talked myself into appreciating Richard's strength behind his convictions, that he was willing to fight for what he believed, even when I was pregnant. I told myself that this was probably nothing more than the ordinary power struggles that many other couples had to face when they were expecting a baby. I wasn't about to let Ellen's opinions crumble the foundation I was building, even if she had known Richard a lot longer than I had.

"No," I had told her. "You're wrong. We're working very hard on this relationship. Richard is making some changes, and I believe they're permanent ones."

"We'll see," she said.

I was shaken by our conversation, and on the way to my couple's therapy appointment, try as I might, I couldn't dismiss Ellen's words. What if Richard distanced himself from me once the baby was born? Would he abandon me? How could I raise a child all alone with no emotional support? I began to create threatening scenarios where Richard was busy with work all day, then he'd come home and play with Gregory and completely ignore me. My feelings were hurt by what he hadn't even done. My heart closed and started hardening toward him. I spilled it out in our session, and as soon as I was finished, Larry, our therapist, burst into laughter. I was shocked and a little bit angry at his reaction.

"Boy," Larry said. "You tell a good scary story!"

"What do you mean?" I asked him. He obviously had not understood how important and real this was to me.

"I mean just what I said," he said in a more serious tone. "Listen to what you said. You're basing your feelings and your behavior on fears that you created with your mind. They have nothing to do with reality or the present circumstances. Can you see how you're scaring yourself?"

I nodded, a sense of relief coming over me. Feeling a little bit silly, I placed my hands on my belly and rubbed in a clockwise circular motion. I mentally spoke to the baby. "Don't worry. We are going to be okay," I reassured him silently. "I'll sort it out and find out all about these scary stories." The ache in my back eased up, and I imagined golden green light surrounding all of us. Larry's voice brought me back into the room.

"If I were you," he said, "I'd save some of those stories for Halloween."

I smiled in spite of myself. Richard, Larry, and I spent the rest of the hour discussing the phenomena of creating scary stories, how susceptible we are to them, and how easy it is to behave in reaction to ideas that aren't real.

I agreed to stay aware of how I was doing this. For the next several weeks, I watched my mind fabricate its daily routine of scary stories, an intricate web of illusion that would inevitably catch me. On my way to work, I would concoct a story about having a flat tire on the freeway and then escalate it to mass murderers abducting me. My imagination knew no bounds; it was impressive how detailed and fantastic the scenarios would be, and I began to understand why life seemed so fraught with danger and anxieties.

With my newfound awareness, I worked on intervening in my own tales with statements like, "Oh, another scary story." I caught them as often as I could, and slowly I began to disengage from the illusions and ground myself in what was real. Scary stories were a prominent thread in the fabric of negativity that I had woven around myself. The more I unraveled it, the freer I became.

# 12

# SHIELDS TO THE FOUR DIRECTIONS

I PAID LITTLE ATTENTION TO LYNN'S WARNINGS ABOUT
my labor. I remembered she had said that the baby
might hold on, but I decided that would not be the case.
I would have a smooth birth with no complications. How
could it be any other way when I had done so many
years of meditation, breathwork, and all-around shamanism? I had read about spiritually attuned women who
gave birth with great ease. I saw myself as one of them.

Lynn knew that I was preparing for a natural birth
without drugs, and she encouraged me to do so. At the
same time, she reminded me that there was no glory in
suffering. She told me not to hesitate to ask for drugs if I
needed them. I half-listened; I had set my mind that my
spirituality would provide me with an ecstatic birth experience, and I would hear of nothing else. In fact, I fore-
saw the challenge of natural childbirth bringing me into
deeper levels of my primal female self. I was ready to be
transformed into a fuller woman, in touch with the mysteries of creation and regeneration.

Since I had become pregnant, I had never felt so whole
or complete. Attending to my daily tasks while life was

forming and expanding inside of me was euphoric. I was a willing container for an entire magical mini-universe, and I anticipated that these feelings would stay with me forever, that the birth process would make them a permanent part of who I was.

Richard and I agreed to have the baby in a birthing center located across the street from the hospital. I had wanted a home birth, but I opted for the birthing center because the possibility of rare complications, however remote, had to be considered. Although I was confident that my birth experience would be blessed, I had to make sure that I was taking every possible precaution without being traditional. You couldn't get much safer than having a hospital right across the street.

The birthing center required that every future parent preregister with the hospital and take the maternity tour, just in case. I always had believed hospitals to be dangerous places where personal rights and needs were disregarded and people were treated like numbers. I didn't want an institutional mentality surrounding my child's birth, but Richard and I took the tour because we had to. I shuddered when we were led down the hallway toward the operating room where cesarean sections were performed. The room itself was wall-to-wall stainless steel, and I didn't want to be there. I tugged at Richard's sleeve, indicating that I wanted to leave the tour early. He gratefully accommodated me, not liking it any better than I did. Before we left, I made it clear to the attending administrator that if any complications arose, I was to be consulted every step of the way. I was glad to leave those hallways and returning there was not a part of my plan.

Massage class, however, was in the plan, and I learned ways of dealing with labor to facilitate a smooth and easy delivery. I cleansed myself physically by eating nourishing foods and drinking raspberry tea. I understood that one of the most challenging experiences of my life was coming up, and if I were well prepared, the labor might serve as an opportunity for me to take my power. I hoped to be one with the Great Mother. I imagined connecting with the lineage of millions of women throughout time who had given birth.

I spent quiet time contemplating and envisioning the Mother presence. I began to put into words those qualities within myself that I wanted to birth along with my son. Grace, gratitude, health, harmony, hope, love, openness, boundaries, balance, and blessings were on the list.

In my last month, I called upon my girlfriend Bonnie to be with me while I did a shamanic fire ceremony. I created a medicine circle and asked Bonnie to sit inside of it with me to represent feminine support. I built a crackling fire in the center and sat down in the east while I asked Bonnie to sit in the north. I began my ceremony with words and prayers, offering my emotional and psychic blockages as a sacrifice to the flames.

"I now offer my fears to the fire," I announced. "All that stands in my way, my doubts, my insecurities, my pain and suffering, my negativity, all that no longer serves me and gets in the way of the possibility of my perfect connection with the Great Mother. Fire Spirit, please receive me now and burn up all of my impurities in your great power."

Into the fire I threw scraps of paper on which I had written symbols of my negativity. I watched them burn until they were nothing more than ash. "I pray for the beauty and power of the Great Mother to enter my life and connect me with the ancient stream that sustains creation. I pray for the openness to receive love and the ability to express that love with warmth and tenderness. I ask for the energy and presence of the Sisterhood of the Shields to permeate my life. I express my profound gratitude for the many blessings I have received on my shamanic path. May these blessings translate into the world in a healing manifestation."

The flames lit up Bonnie's eyes until they appeared almost transparent. I realized I had asked for a lot and I was filled with a sudden dread. The truth was that the power and energy of the primordial feminine scared me. I wondered if Bonnie could see it in my face. "Bonnie, I need to talk to you," I told her. "It's about something that happened to me many years ago."

Bonnie nodded, sitting quietly, her legs crossed beneath her. I took a deep breath, shivering as I exhaled, preparing to tell my story.

"Several years before I started my work with Lynn, I read her book *Flight of the Seventh Moon*. She talks about the process of creating shields to the cardinal points of a compass, and awakening the corresponding energies asso-

ciated with each of the four directions. These four directions are the building blocks for the medicine wheels,
which are a way to know yourself and move closer to
enlightenment.

"I wanted to do medicine work myself—I knew that I
needed it for my soul—but I had no teacher and no idea
how to find one. Trying to contact Lynn seemed out of
the question, and even if I could have found her, I knew
nothing about shamanism, so I was sure she would have
no interest in seeing me. I decided to use Lynn's experiences from the book to create my own shields to the
four directions. Over the next few months, I followed
her descriptions as best I could to construct the shields
with the ability to awaken the corresponding qualities in
myself."

"How did you know what to do?" Bonnie asked.

"She included in the book the lessons that her teachers had taught her, and I read them carefully. For example, Agnes Whistling Elk, Lynn's main teacher, said that to
make a shield in the proper manner, you have to destroy
your own personal conflicting parts. I thought about that
and tried to interpret it for myself. Agnes also said that a
shield is protective medicine and a mirror for the soul. I
followed the principles as closely as I could and when
I actually made them, I improvised."

Bonnie's face showed some awe and a little disbelief.
"Improvised? What do you mean?"

"I started out with an embroidery hoop. I stretched
white canvas across the face, and then I went to the

beach—you know, the one at Moss Landing. I sat facing the south in the middle of all those powerful rocks, and I meditated. When I turned my head to face a certain angle, even with my eyes closed the light was blinding. I opened my eyes and saw that the sun, reflected in a pool of water, shone like lightning shooting off the rocks at different angles. I felt that power was there, showing me that lightning was one of my personal southern symbols.

"I pricked my finger, squeezed out a drop of blood, and I used the blood to draw a lightning bolt down the center of the face of the shield. Then I found some string, which I sewed onto the bottom of the shield in a way that represented ocean waves. At the top of the shield, I pierced small holes for the light to come through, and those were the stars. Then I did the ceremony to awaken it."

"What about the other shields? Were they all different?"

"Yes. It took me many months to finish all four, and I awakened each individually as I completed them one at a time. Once I went to the ocean and laid my shields on the water. For the west, I buried it at the base of a tree and danced around it. With each shield, I connected with different nature symbols, placed them on the shield, and then awakened them with ceremony.

"Lynn wrote about having attained a completeness within herself after finishing her shielding process. It was then that she was initiated into the Sisterhood of the Shields. I wanted that level of completeness; I wanted to feel that whole."

"I understand, Jen," Bonnie answered. "I guess we all

want that. I certainly do, but I never defined it as clearly as you did or went about it with such intent."

"It was amazing how much I felt with each ceremony and how specific the feelings were. After I awakened my southern shield, for several weeks the qualities of trust and innocence ran through me."

"What do you mean?" Bonnie asked.

"I mean that in many ways I felt the wonder of being a child. The most mundane everyday things like getting out of bed and making breakfast seemed as if they were happening for the first time. It was as if my past experience was wiped out and everything was brand new. Every sunset was a miracle. Colors were brighter; I took nothing for granted. It was amazing, and it was constant. Every moment of life was an adventure."

"It sounds fabulous!"

"It was. And it was also unsettling because my perception was so altered; it was a little disorienting, but I loved it anyway. Next, I moved to the west and made my western shield. The west is the direction associated with transformation, death, and rebirth. After I buried the shield, awakened it, and retrieved it, my dreams started showing up in Technicolor. I had never had such lucid visions."

"What kind of visions? Were they different from dreams?" Bonnie wanted to know.

"They were different from any dreams I had ever had. They weren't just pictures, although there were some strong images in them. I kept seeing this ancient native woman who talked to me about balancing the light and the dark. I remember her telling me to find my inner balance by meditating on the twilight. I never forgot, and to this day, the setting sun reminds me of that woman and her teaching."

Telling the story seemed to have brought back the feelings. "You know, Bonnie, when I tell you about it, I can't really describe the force because these visions would piggyback one on the next. Before I could even begin to think about a new thought, another would be right there. They overlapped in a split second."

"That sounds like the transitions stage in birth, doesn't it?"

"It sure does, and I often wonder if birth will be anything like that. Some mornings, I'd wake up with answers that I needed, and I knew when I was about to run into people because I would dream about them the night before. It was exciting, but I was getting weary because my dreamtime was so active. I would wake up feeling that I had been very busy in my sleep. And yet, I was surprised at how much energy I had.

"After I constructed my shield for the north, it seemed that my compassion toward myself greatly increased and, along with it, my tolerance for other people's problems. I found myself listening better and caring more. I felt wiser in my decision making and clearer in my ability to make choices that would benefit the larger picture. This was a beautiful experience because as my inner strength increased, my doubts diminished."

"I'd really like that for myself. Maybe I should read the book," Bonnie said, a sense of urgency in her voice.

"Wait for the end of the story. It may not be what you think. Finally I made my eastern shield. I came to understand that this power allows you to test the institutions and laws that are already in place to see if they are truly serving the people or if they are working against the common good. It was during this time that I seemed to be doing everything backward and then I ended up in the right place."

Bonnie laughed. "I think that happens to me every day."

"Then you know exactly what I'm talking about. So after I had awakened each shield individually and felt the energies of each of the directions, I had an idea. What would happen if I awakened the four shields together in one ceremony? Wouldn't that give me the sense of wholeness I was looking for? I decided to try it. I took two weeks off from work and headed out to Arizona."

"Boy, you were really serious about this, weren't you?"

"I really was. I timed my trip with the February full moon. I arrived two days early and explored the countryside to find my ceremonial spot. I found a mesa that was laid out in a circular shape. I sat in the center of the circle, envisioning dramatic cloud formations passing at intervals through the light of the full moon, with a wild animal or two coming out of the bushes to befriend me and add power to my ceremony. I could hardly wait.

"The night of the actual ceremony brought a torrential

downpour. I trudged my way through red mud to my chosen 'perfect' spot and spread out my shields in front of me. With rivulets of water pouring down my face, I watched red dirt begin to bleed onto my precious shields. I was unable to strike a match so I couldn't burn the cleansing herbs. I did the ceremony anyway. The rain soaked my clothes, and the February cold seeped into my bones. I offered my prayers to the Great Spirit and each of the four directions. I tried to include every aspect of sacredness I could think of: the sun, the moon, the stars, endless space, Mother Earth, Father Sky.

"The more it rained, the more my list of spiritual intentions grew. Basically, my prayers were for self-realization, and I tried to invoke each and every facet of enlightenment. I was so cold and uncomfortable and disappointed; still I prayed and cried until my tears and the water flowing down my hair and face were one and the same. But nothing happened. The moonlight was thickly covered with dark storm clouds, and no wild animals appeared. Do you remember the Charlie Brown cartoons about Halloween?"

"You mean when everybody gets candy and he gets a rock?" Bonnie asked.

"Exactly. I felt like Charlie Brown. 'I'm getting a rock,' I muttered to myself that night. I couldn't understand why I didn't feel anything, no power, no spirit, no ceremonial energy whatsoever. In each of my individual ceremonies, I had felt a solid rush of adrenaline passing through my system. I had felt invigorated. I knew that something had happened because I had felt cleansed and alive and everything looked different. Even garbage took on beauty and new meaning. I hadn't minded the nausea and headaches as the different aspects of my body were cleansing. But tonight it all felt dead. I was chilled to the bone on this stormy winter night for no reason. Disgusted, I decided to leave.

"I headed back to the hotel to change out of my soaked clothes and to get a bite to eat. I drove to a nearby restaurant. I ordered, and while thinking about 'getting a rock,' I suddenly began to feel lightheaded. Then I felt as if intense sheets of electrical fields were imploding my system. I looked down to my left at the carpet beside my table, and the floor appeared to be rolling like ocean waves. I couldn't eat, so I got up and somehow managed to drive myself back to the motel.

"I stayed there for three days and nights while spirit with the intensity of the rainstorm on the mesa poured through my body. I was simultaneously hot and cold. I shook and trembled while I had visions that were kinesthetic. I'd feel a popping at the back of my neck, and then I'd have a sudden realization. I saw that my need to be right kept people at a distance and blocked love from fully expressing itself in my life. Then my heart beat faster. At times it would beat so fast, I thought a freight train was running through me. It took my breath away. When I could breathe again, I was filled up with wonderfully tender and compassionate feelings. Through all of it, I was nauseated, and my entire body ached. It was so excruciating,

I could feel pain in the individual hairs on my head. There was nothing I could do but stay with it until it passed."

"Were you all alone?"

"At first, but I called a friend who flew out to be with me. When I could sit up without constant nausea, she drove me home."

"Was that the end of it?"

"No. Over the next several months, intermittent bouts of this electrical field would rush through me with no warning. Strange things began to happen."

"What kinds of strange things?" Bonnie asked, mesmerized by my story.

"Please don't think I'm nuts, but I could smell people's feelings."

Bonnie looked at me with disbelief. "How can anyone smell feelings?"

"I don't know how. I just could. And it wasn't much fun. I was a therapist working in a hospital where there was a lot of sickness, fear, and mistrust. Let me tell you, these emotions don't smell very good. But my new olfactory gifts were a great help in diagnosing and understanding people's feelings. And there was a pattern to it. For example, victim energy smelled like stale perfume. Anger smelled like burnt corn. Fear smelled like baby poop. So even when my clients were confused about their own feelings, I wasn't.

"Emotions flew at me from all directions, and my nervous system was being flooded and overstimulated. I

walked into a bank one day, and I had to sit down because I was overwhelmed by the emotional pain in the
room. At times like these, I wished I could undo it all, but
it was too late. I had to learn to live with it. I struggled to
integrate this new awareness. And I have."

Bonnie uncrossed her legs and stood up. "I understand
why you're afraid of the energy now. Have you ever told
Lynn about it?"

"Oh yes. She called it a 'kundalini awakening.' I read
about it in a book by an Eastern guru named Swami
Muktananda. He describes kundalini as the primordial
Shakti or cosmic energy that lies coiled in the sexual center of every human being. He says that when that energy
is awakened, it begins to move upward and create purifi-
cations. These cleansings are generally good, they allow a
person to endure the energy of higher states of consciousness. I guess I just awakened mine too quickly, and
my body wasn't prepared to handle it all."

"Well, don't worry," Bonnie assured me. "It won't happen again like that. You've done your work and, besides,
Gregory won't allow it."

I patted my tummy and smoothed the outline of
Gregory's growing body. Soon he would be too big to fit
his cramped quarters. Bonnie and I both smiled and
walked toward the car. Bonnie took my hand, and as I
looked up into the sky, I gave a prayer of thanks for the
waxing moon, a warm dry night, and a good close friend
by my side.

# 13

## CONNECTION TO THE PRIMORDIAL

THE NIGHT BEFORE MY DUE DATE, WHILE WATCHING television beside Richard, I felt a gushing from between my legs. I looked down, to see the couch beneath me soaked. My water had broken. Even though I was so close to the designated time, I was still amazed. I hadn't felt anything and had had no physical warnings.

"My water just broke," I told Richard, quite matter-of-factly.

He looked up in disbelief. "Are you kidding?"

"No. It just happened. I can feel it leaking onto the sofa."

We sat there paralyzed, staring at the television. All those birthing classes, all the mental and physical preparations, and we had no idea what to do.

"Are you sure your water broke?" he asked me again.

"Yes, I'm sure. It's still leaking, and I'm having small contractions."

"What shall we do?"

"I'm going to pray first. Then I'll figure out what to do."

I prayed for a while, and then Richard insisted that we lie down in bed, but sleep was impossible. Hours passed. I got up and paced. A drowsy Richard grabbed the stopwatch, valiantly struggling to keep his eyes open to time the contractions. He finally succumbed to sleep while I got into a warm shower to ease my discomfort, wondering how anyone could go unconscious at a time like this. Rushes of water washed me on the outside while a light stream continued to drip from my insides. I'm on my own, I thought. This thing is happening to me, to my body and nobody else's. Better not expect anything from anybody, especially Richard.

At my midwife Wanda's suggestion, I spent most of the night in a rhythm, alternately taking showers and then walking back and forth, with fairly consistent contractions. I waited for them to get closer together and more intense, but at 7:30 the next morning, they suddenly stopped. I was surprised but since I had been up all night, I was too tired to analyze it. I tried to sleep, but each time I began to doze, a vigorous solitary contraction would jettison me awake.

"I give up. You win." I said to my belly. I walked into the kitchen where Richard was having coffee. His sleep had been interrupted all throughout the night, and he looked tired. I, on the other hand, had a sudden burst of energy. "Why don't we go Christmas shopping?" I suggested. He burst into laughter.

"Jennifer, you have to be patient. Call Bonnie to come

and keep you company. I don't think shopping is the best idea right now."

Bonnie came by, and while Richard went upstairs to nap, Bonnie and I took a walk. "Just think, Jen," she said. "By this time tomorrow, you'll be a mother."

I looked at her incredulously. Then I stopped at the base of a giant redwood tree and sat. Acutely aware of my intermittent contractions, I envisioned cords of golden white light coming off of my hands and feet. I gestured as if throwing the cords deep into the earth, grounding myself and connecting to the Great Mother. I prayed for her wisdom and her help in centering myself.

When we got back, Richard was up. We got into the car to go see my obstetrician while Bonnie took her turn napping on the couch. It seemed as if everybody was getting to rest but me. Wanda met us at Dr. Seymour's office, concerned about infection since my water had already broken. She joined us in the examination room.

"Your water has resealed itself," the doctor announced, looking rather disinterested. "And you're not dilated. Not at all."

"But how could that be?" I asked him, "I'm having contractions."

He shrugged and turned to his desk to look at some papers. His attitude suggested that neither my labor, my baby, nor I were of any significance to him whatsoever. He seemed to be annoyed. This was not how I had envisioned birth. I was a medicine woman. Where was the

magic, where was the power, where was my perfect shamanic experience?

After another night of relentless labor, at 8:00 A.M. the
phone rang. "That was Wanda," Richard told me. "She
said to come into the birthing center."

I inhaled sharply, holding onto my stomach, feeling a
contraction pass through me. When it was finished, I
sighed relief. "Thank God, it's time," I said.

"No, I don't think so. She didn't say to bring your
things. She just said to come in for a checkup."

"It's time. I know it is. Go get my bag."

"How do you know? I don't think that's what she
meant. I talked to her. You didn't."

I couldn't believe he was arguing with me. Why couldn't
he defer to me just this once? After more protesting, he
agreed to take my suitcase, and when Wanda met us in
the lobby, she ushered me into the birthing room. I settled in, unpacking some sage and crumbling several leaves
between my fingers. The pungent scent filled the room.
I prayed that the sage would purify the environment and
asked that I might connect with the Sisterhood of the
Shields. A sense of calm overtook me. I sniffed the lin-
gering smell of sage on my fingertips, and I knew that I
was not alone, that Lynn and this group of self-realized
women were with me in my experience. I sat on the bed
to gather my focus. I was relieved to finally be here, but
everything seemed to be moving so slowly.

Suddenly Wanda tore into the room. "We're running
out of time," she said. "Your contractions are too weak,

and I'm afraid of infection," she said in a chastising voice. Tears swelled in the corners of my eyes. I turned my face away so she would not be able to see the impact her words had made on me. Then a large contraction shook me, followed by another and yet another. A strange involuntary sound like the moo of a giant cow escaped from my mouth. "Is that strong enough for you?" I thought, embarrassed at the noise I had made. Where had that primitive sound come from? My body continued to contract, shaking hard. Richard took my arm, and together we walked outside as I mooed and grunted my way through the next two hours. I chuckled in between moos.

"What's funny?" Richard asked.

"It's just the irony of it all," I managed to say. I had wanted a direct experience of the Great Mother. Well, here it was, complete with sound effects. With a smile on my face, I noticed that, all in all, I was doing pretty well.

When I returned to the room, I was three centimeters dilated. I felt accomplished, but the others were concerned at how long I had been in labor. With a frown on his face, the doctor spoke quietly to Wanda. She walked away and then returned with a long object that looked like a large knitting needle. With no warning, Doctor Seymour inserted the object inside of me and poked at my water. It broke open and warm fluid gushed out. I burst into tears. They were treating me like an object with no intelligence or feelings. Dr. Seymour looked chagrined and then apologized through clenched teeth for not warning me. His pager went off, and he left, predicting that my labor would speed up now.

Wave after wave of contractions began to shudder through me. It took all of my concentration to cope. I shifted and turned, stood and sat, trying every position I could imagine. The strength and intensity of the pain were overwhelming, and I imagined that my back was ground down to particles of dust. When Bonnie arrived, cheerfully announcing that she had seen another couple from our birthing class, I wanted to scream, "Who the fuck cares?" Instead I muttered, "I couldn't care less." She got the message; I was beyond social niceties.

At 8:00 on my third night of labor, a gentle rain fell outside the window while my contractions were ten to fifteen seconds apart. There was no recovery time; intense ripping sensations seared through my back and abdomen. I was claustrophobic; I began to think I might die. I could not see myself moving beyond the moment. "For birth to happen, some part of you has to die," Wanda said. She looked at me, waiting for a reply.

"I *am* dying," I told her.

I called on Lynn, using the sacred name I had given her. "Spirit Woman! Agnes! Ruby! I need your help! Give me strength!"

A contraction hit. I retched and threw up all over the carpet. Wanda, ever the bearer of bad news, told me that the lip of my cervix was swelling, inhibiting further opening. My uterus went berserk at the information, with a series of quick, hard contractions, one upon the other. I needed help, real help. "I want to go to the hospital," I groaned. "Get Dr. Seymour and tell him."

Wanda didn't move. She looked flustered for a moment and then said, "I can't get him. His kids beeped him and he went home. The electricity went out at his house from the rainstorm."

"He left?" I screamed. "Call him on his car phone. Tell him to call the hospital for me. I have to be admitted right now!"

Amazed at the strength of my voice, Wanda flew to the phone. I could hardly believe my forcefulness and my ability to give orders in such a state, but something else had taken over. I felt close to death and was determined to get myself and my baby to a safe place. I yelled to the people around me to hurry up. They seemed to be moving in slow motion.

I don't how I got there, but in several minutes, I was in the elevator of the hospital down the street. The door opened onto the maternity ward and I fell into the hallway. "Please help!" I screamed to the nurse.

Richard looked at me with embarrassment on his face. "This is a natural process. You don't need to scream," he said.

"This is beyond natural," I snarled.

The anesthesiologist came in and hooked me up to an epidural. My body numbed. The room filled with the soft chirping of an infant's heartbeat coming from the baby monitor. Pitocin dripped through my I.V. to increase the efficiency of my contractions. It was a blessing to be unaware of them after three solid days and nights. But I also felt outcast and lonely, surrounded by metal instruments and the sounds of technology. The nurse rolled me on my side and told me to rest. I suddenly remembered Lynn's warning.

"The baby loves being close to your heart. He doesn't want to leave. He might want to hold on because he doesn't want to lose that connection with you. If the labor stops midway, tell him he can have your love on the outside, too."

Facing the wall, I was acutely aware that the baby was still inside of me and that would have to change. One hour later, I was fully dilated. They discontinued the epidural and told me to push. Now I could have my spiritual experience; I could forget the panic and awkwardness of the last days and go into the magic. With my last ounce of strength, I pulled up on the birthing bar and pushed, ready for the miracle to unfold.

"I can see the baby's head. Keep pushing," Wanda encouraged.

"Move into the light," I silently told the baby. "There's a heart connection for you on the outside, too. You're gonna be born tonight, one way or the other." How had Lynn known that my labor would be this challenging?

After I had pushed for two grueling hours, Wanda, in her inimitable fashion, declared, "This baby is not moving down." I slumped back. Wanda went down the hall to get Dr. Seymour. Droopy-eyed from his interrupted slumber, he examined me. "Jennifer, we've tried all the options. The baby's head is not a good fit for your pelvis. I thought this might happen. We have to do a cesarean."

I reeled with conflicting emotions. I was furious that I had gone through such trauma and agony for nothing. At the same time, if the head was not a good fit, then it was not my fault. I had done nothing to cause the outcome of a cesarean birth. And yet, I felt that I had failed as a spiritually attuned woman who assuredly would have a sensuous birth process at best, and at worst, an uncomplicated one. I finally let go; there was nothing left to do.

It was after 2:00 A.M. when they wheeled me into the dreaded stainless steel operating room. Amid my exhaustion, disappointment, and feelings of failure, Gregory was cut from my uterus. He looked beautiful to me, but his first yell grated on my frayed nerves. His cries continued. A solitary tear ran down my cheek. My mouth was dry as a bone. My body trembled and shook violently as the medications wore off. Richard held my hand and fed me ice chips. I was too weak to hold my own baby. I watched Bonnie cuddling him, swaying and cooing to him. He responded to her gentleness, and his cries subsided. Encouraged by her success with him, grateful for the peace, I dropped off to sleep, no longer caring how it had happened, simply relieved that it was over.

# 14

## PRAGMATIC SHAMANISM

TWO DAYS AFTER MY SURGERY, I LEFT THE HOSPITAL. The doctor agreed to discharge Gregory and me, providing Richard would diligently attend to us. Richard gave his word. I wanted to be at home with my family, and it appeared that Richard wanted that also. The doctor gave me strict instructions not to walk up the stairs and to rest as much as possible. From what Richard told the doctor, I would be able to count on him while I healed from the surgery and got used to caring for my new son.

When the doctor left the room, Richard and I had a fight about how best to organize the departure from the hospital. I had little strength at this point, and the argument took away both my confidence in Richard's help and any reserves of energy I had tucked away. He was quiet on the drive home, and I was grateful for it; the ordeal of getting myself and Gregory into the car had exhausted me.

As soon as he had helped me and his newborn son into the house, Richard left me standing in the kitchen and ran upstairs. I was glad to be back home, but I felt abandoned as I awkwardly shifted my weight onto a kitchen chair and listened to the floorboards creaking above me. Richard was walking around; he was probably doing some last-minute preparations in the nursery. I wondered why he was bothering with this now; we wouldn't be able to use the nursery until I could walk upstairs. I sat and waited, feeling forlorn and helpless, lost in my own home.

In a few minutes Richard bounded down the stairs, walked into the kitchen and said, "Listen, Jennifer. I really need to do some Christmas shopping. I never expected the birth to take so much time. If you don't mind, I'll skip getting your present right now until I can give it some more thought, but I have to get something for my mother and my brother. I'm sure you understand."

I nodded in compliance. I was too weak to do anything else. The truth was that I was terrified to be alone with Gregory in my weakened state, but I was more terrified to try to talk to Richard about it. I knew that another argument would completely debilitate me. He carried the baby into the living room, placed him in the bassinet, and left. Gregory slept, and I sat on the couch and wept.

I quickly fell into the routine of caring for my son. It became obvious early on that, once again, I was on my own. It was just as Ellen had predicted; Richard became withdrawn, and he was absent a great deal of the time. But even during this difficult postpartum period, my son brought me endless joy. Gregory's needs, although simple, were all-consuming, and as I healed from my operation and the exhaustion of a long labor, I was astonished to find that I was able to be there for him.

When Gregory was two weeks old, at the beginning of the new year, I had a medicine dream. I was at a huge gathering with Lynn and all of her apprentices. The atmosphere was festive and carnival-like. Teepees were set up in a clearing spotted with cedar trees. Huge fires blazed beneath cooking pots that billowed with steam. The aromas of exotic foods were enticing, and I eagerly anticipated the celebratory meal.

I waited for my time with Lynn, chatting with some of the women while a ceremony was being prepared. Drumming reached a crescendo and then receded while the air filled with clouds of smoke from cedar, sage, and sweetgrass. Just as I was beginning to wonder if my turn would ever come, Lynn approached me. I felt a tugging sensation, and I opened myself to her while, with her intent, she pulled doubt out of my body. The release was so dramatic, I felt the shift happen on every level. Physically, I experienced a sensation of lightness and well-being. When I awoke, I was thrilled to find that the buoyancy and joy were still there.

My physical healing was moving along, but I had a hard time accepting the C-section. I struggled with my belief that if I had done everything right and lived my life from a true spiritual perspective, only good things would happen to me. During the months that I carried Gregory, I had assumed that because of my shamanic work, I was invincible, immune to certain types of problems. I had to face the fact that this clearly was not true. I felt embarrassed and ashamed, especially in front of other people, that I had failed to bear my child naturally. After all my spiritual talk, I had to face the truth that I had needed medical intervention to give birth. I judged myself for it, and I expected that other people must be judging me, too.

When Gregory was six weeks old, I took my first bath. Baths always had been a solace to me, and as I luxuriated in the tub, looking down at my scarred, flabby stomach, I remembered the last time I had bathed. I had been beautifully swollen with pregnancy then, in awe of the miracle happening inside of me, anticipating the ecstasy of birth. I got out of the tub with tears in my eyes and, still soaking wet, went to find Richard. I broke into sobs when I saw him.

"Richard," I moaned. "I can't take it anymore. I'm tired of not sleeping, my nipples are sore from constant nursing, my stomach hurts from the surgery, and just look at my stretched-out belly! It shakes like Jell-O!"

He stared at me while I complained, begging him with my eyes to say something to make me feel better. He blew up in anger. "Stop feeling sorry for yourself, Jennifer!" His words were like a slap in the face. He went on, leading with his cold, calculating intellect that I had learned to detest. "You know there's a part of you that is very self-pitying. That's what I'm hearing from you now. I've been meaning to say this to you, and I didn't want to upset you so soon after the birth. But obviously you really need to hear it; it's for your own good."

I cried silently while he lectured me about sacrifices and parenting, using himself as the good example. I couldn't believe he thought he was beyond reproach. Where had he been for the last six weeks? Hadn't he seen how much I was giving day and night? Didn't I have the right to break down for a moment?

"Here's the bottom line," he said. "If you're overwhelmed by being a parent, then you have a problem. Go to a therapist, because you obviously need help." With that, he turned on his heel and left the room.

I wiped the tears from my eyes and, without thinking, tugged the wedding band from my left hand and slipped it into the drawer of my nightstand. Then I went on with my day.

In a conversation with Lynn on the phone, I told her all about the birth, leaving out the parts about how poorly Richard had treated me. I wasn't ready to deal with it. I wanted to handle the trauma first, and Lynn gave me exactly what I needed. Her voice was soothing and her kinds words consoled me. As I finished relaying my saga about the pain and exhaustion, she said, "Jennifer, go into your body and tell me what you find there right now."

"There's a strange kind of buzzing in my head," I told her.

"That's a barrier you created to suppress the trauma. It was a good defense for you once. You needed it at the time, but you don't need it anymore. Imagine you're spreading a healing balm all throughout your mind, especially where the noise is coming from. I'll do it with you."

I did as she suggested and felt an immediate release of tension.

"I'll pray for you tonight, honey. Just remember that you did fine. Nobody could have handled it better."

Her words were like sweet music. I used them to help me. The more I concentrated on healing my mind concerning the birth and the C-section, the more I accepted the fact that life happens on its own terms. I saw that being spiritual doesn't protect anyone from life's tragedies or joys. Following a medicine path was not about to alleviate life's challenges. Rather, it would help me to cope wisely with them.

As the weeks passed, my acceptance of my difficult labor and the subsequent surgery softened and humanized me. With time, I began to appreciate that I had handled a crisis well and that my shamanic training had not failed me. It had supported me all the way through and would continue to do so.

# 15

## CLAN OF THE WHISTLING ELK

GREGORY WAS FIVE MONTHS OLD WHEN I PACKED him up along with his favorite baby-sitter, my sister Susie, to join me at Lynn's yearly medicine gathering of the clan of the Whistling Elk. As usual, it was taking place up in Joshua Tree. This year was the year of the drum, and the theme of the gathering was "Drumming the Sacred Drummer."

I had little knowledge about the deeper purpose for creating a drum. I only knew some of the peripheral ideas about drumming and its relationship to sound. Agnes had told Lynn, "Sound is what holds the world together. When you know how to make the sound of a desired object, it appears to you." It made me think of sound as something like cosmic glue.

I wondered how drumming might help me in my day-to-day life, especially with my clients. Sound played an important part in my therapy; it was a vehicle of communication in which a person could help me to understand how he or she felt. I deliberately used speech to shift a client's awareness and perspective. Sometimes, my choice of words and the intent with which I spoke them seemed to pierce through my clients' veils of half-truths. At other times, when my choice of words was less skillful, I felt that the sounds bounced off or became distorted in the muck of someone's unresolved personal history. I was anxious to find more effective ways to use sound, and I hoped that this weekend would give me more tools.

We arrived on a Wednesday afternoon at the Palm Springs Airport. I rented a car, and the three of us drove for forty-five minutes up into the hills, passing through Yucca Valley and Morongo Valley and finally arriving in the little town of Joshua Tree in the high desert. As we pulled into the driveway to the Institute for Mentalphysics, where the gathering was traditionally held, I noted the unusual architecture, mostly designed by Frank Lloyd Wright, in which the various buildings seemed to flow directly into the desert surrounding them. When we stopped the car and I breathed in the fragrance of desert cedar and chaparral, a scent so strong and particular to that place, I knew I was home.

I completed the required registration for the workshop, and then we went to dinner. I was very hungry; I wolfed down a hearty meal of Mexican food, including two enchiladas with plenty of rice and refried beans. Then we checked into the hotel. We all slept well that night, and when I awakened to the sound of birdcalls and the scampering of desert creatures, I was happy. We left early for the meeting house, and just outside the front of the institute, I found a private grove surrounded by rhododendron bushes. With several blankets and a foam pad, I made a small shaded nest for Gregory, where he and Susie spent most of the next four days.

Many of the women had brought their drums from home, so the air was filled with drumming accompanied by the shaking of rattles until Lynn entered the room. During the first day, in what we called our "dreamtime work," Lynn took us on a power animal journey. I had done this in the first workshop I ever attended with Lynn, as had many of the other women. She had explained that this journey was one of the most basic and important ones in our shamanic practice. "The search for your power animal is a search for your original nature," she had said. "We will travel back into primordial time through a tunnel into the lower world of the power animals and ancestors. It is there that you will find what you are looking for." I had found a gigantic two hundred–pound apricot-coated English mastiff. This magnificent dog represents the loyal guardian and protector. He is also the guardian of the ancient secrets. Along with the horse, the great dog guides the way to the higher levels of consciousness, expressing his commitment to service for the greater good of the person or community he protects.

Now, we were repeating the meditation, and I was eager to see what would happen. "No matter how many times you take this journey, it is always good," Lynn said. "This is the way you strengthen your bond with your power animal and your original nature. Bonding with your animal is essential; it protects and guides you in your work as a healer while it keeps you physically strong.

"So many of you have changed profoundly over this last year." Lynn paused and looked around at particular women in the room. "It is quite possible that some of you may find a new power animal. This is natural. Remember, there is no jealousy in the world of true power, only an exchange of love and strength. One animal is as powerful and valid as the next, so free yourselves to discover what is there. Don't resist change. No preconceptions. Uncover your true selves, for it is there that power lives. Relax and breathe deeply."

A solitary drum began to sound. My eyes felt heavy, and I allowed them to fall shut. I had no idea if it were Lynn beating the drum, an assistant, or a being from another world. Lynn's soothing voice rose up over the rhythmic beats. "Imagine you are walking across a grassy meadow. Birds-of-paradise and chrysanthemums are on all sides; their fragrance drifts on the gentle breezes that caress you along your path. Just ahead of you, a pond shimmers in the sun like liquid silver. Find a comfortable place to sit beside the pond as I lead you through your journey into the lower world."

The drumming continued in its steady rhythm, filling the room with a tangible potency.

"Enter the pond," Lynn encouraged. "Submerge your body and your head. It's okay. You can breathe beneath the water's surface. Dive to the bottom and look in front of you. Do you see the opening? This is the feminine, the entrance to the tunnel. It is a sacred 'see-pa-poo.' I had never heard those words, but as she uttered them, a ripple of energy shuddered up my spine.

"Now see a grassy plain. It's at the end of your journey through the tunnel. It will look different to each of you. Some of you may see many animals there, and others will have to call out to your power animal to present itself. If you see more than one, your particular power animal will present itself to you from four different sides, each of the four directions. When this happens, I want you to put your arms around your power animal and take him or her up the spiraling tunnel to rest on the shore of the pond. When you're back, sit up, and I'll know that your journey is complete."

The drumming intensified as Lynn's voice faded. With each insistent beat, my consciousness swirled deeper down the luminescent ribbed tunnel. Time seemed to stretch out of proportion, leaving me disoriented, with no idea of when I had begun the journey or when it would end. I felt dizzy, my body twirling and spinning of its own volition. Vertigo threatened to overwhelm me and then, gratefully, I caught sight of the light at the edge of the tunnel. I had the sensation of being tossed out of the tunnel and into a meadow. I sat up to get my bearings, the dizziness very slowly fading away.

When I could focus clearly, I was blinded by the brightness of the vivid colors. I looked to my left, hoping to relieve my eyes, and there was the great dog, his golden-red coat gleaming radiantly, a greenish light emanating from his heart. I swelled with love at the sight of him, feeling his strength, loyalty, and devotion toward me. I lay back and breathed him in, secure in his presence.

Suddenly, there was a great flapping of wings in the air

just above me. For a moment the light was completely obscured and the air around me felt unsettled. Soft feathers brushed against me, compelling me to sit up. A gigantic bald eagle stood before me in all of its magnificence. He was unfamiliar, and I had a difficult time looking at him. It was his bearing; he was regal and mighty, and he pulled me straight into my own center of awareness.

With careful precision, he took flight and circled me, hovering for a moment in each of the four directions, presenting himself to me. My mouth fell open. I wanted to argue that power was mistaken, that this was not my animal. Perhaps he had confused me with someone else. He landed in front of me, and without sounds or words, he soothed my mind and body, smoothing my own ruffled feathers. The great dog joined him, assuring me that I was not losing an ally, I was simply gaining an additional one. I reached toward the eagle. He stood steady. I gathered him in my arms, and he nestled under my chin and shoulder as I journeyed back up the tunnel to the water's edge. Together, we lifted high into the air, and I could feel his instinctive bird nature merging with my own, gifting me with his vision behind my own eyes as we soared over the landscape. No longer able to hold my attention in the other world, I found myself back in the meeting room, elated and, at the same time, spent.

Lynn gave us a break. We had all journeyed, and I wasn't the only one who felt disoriented. I went to my son's nest and nursed him for a little while, soothed by holding him in my arms, awed by my new ally. The eagle! I had certainly changed this year.

I felt refreshed when we reconvened, and I listened intently while Lynn described to us the deeper meaning of drumming. "The physical creation of a personal medicine drum will affect your lives in many ways," she told us. "Drumming transports us from the world of the ordinary to the world of the extraordinary. We ride the currents of sound, which take us into the dimension of power."

We continued the morning with a meditation to find our power animal specifically for drumming medicine. In this journey, we worked with a partner, facing each other, journeying for the other person. When my partner announced my drumming power animal to be the parrot, I laughed because Richard said that when I was startled, I squawked like a parrot.

After lunch, we spent the afternoon creating our drums. In my moments of doubt during the weeks preceding the workshop, I could not fathom how making a drum could change me. As I had gathered the necessary materials, the whole thing seemed stupid, and I wondered if it was all a hoax. "Imagine spending hundreds of dollars to make a drum," I grumbled to myself. "Why don't I just stay home and buy one? Wouldn't that be more sensible?" But now, sitting in a group of similarly focused women at work, as I strung my precious drum together, I imagined the sound of drumming to mimic the pulse of life.

"A drum is like a heartbeat that connects us to the heartbeat of Mother Earth," Lynn told us. "We can use drumming as a vehicle, a way of transporting us to other dimensions."

I felt the materials coming alive in my hands, and I

understood the power in creating it myself. Once again I was grateful that I was here, doing the task before me, allowing myself to understand and integrate more of the sacred teachings. I had invited Susie and Gregory to come inside while we made our drums and Gregory, soothed by the soft feminine energy, fell fast asleep in a corner of the room. Just as I completed the stringing of my drum, Gregory awakened. I went to nurse him with a sense of contentment that I could take care of my son's needs and do my shamanic tasks at the same time.

# 16

# CRACK BETWEEN THE WORLDS

THE NEXT MORNING BEGAN WITH ANOTHER GUIDED journey. Lynn gave us an introduction before we began. "This meditation is about finding the great masters who are no longer manifested on the physical plane. It is about the rainbow bridge created by drumming that will take you into the higher levels of consciousness. When you drum with strong intention in the shaman way, a still point is reached, a point of silence where the drum takes over, moving you beyond thought to where the Great Spirit lives. Among the Sisterhood of the Shields, we refer to this as the crack between the worlds. Let's go there now. Take several deep breaths with me."

We all closed our eyes, and a calm descended upon the room. The sound of tiny bells filled the air behind Lynn's voice. "Take your awareness up through your toes and torso to the top of your head. Now see yourself walking on a deserted beach in a wilderness area. Feel the sand beneath your feet and between your toes, the warmth of the sun on your bare skin. A gentle breeze beckons you to enter the great ocean. Look out into the far distance and remove all of your clothes slowly, piece by piece. Step into the water, walk out for a few minutes, and then dive beneath the surface.

"The bright fish dazzle you. See the bars of light reflecting off the coral reef. Just to your left, notice a large fish moving toward you. As you swim and play, you are delighted to find that you can breathe easily beneath the surface. As you dart up above the surface of the water, you see a dolphin by your side. You hug your new friend, and she begins to swim with you, guiding you on a journey. Jump on her back and allow her to lead you through the waters. The joy and rhythm of her movements will bring you profound peace. Deeper and deeper you move toward the ocean floor until a far-off light catches your eye. As you focus on the light, you begin to perceive a large crystal formation in the distance. You are finding your way to the domain of the ascended masters.

"The closer you get, the more you can see the prismatic colors reflecting off the crystalline form. It is a large building made of clear quartz, and when you reach the entrance, your dolphin guide gently nudges you toward the archway. Touch the solid crystal walls and explore the rooms while the charismatic light fills your inner and outer eye."

Lynn's voice, more and more diffused by the clarity of the images in my mind's eye, was replaced by the sound of a loud horn. I swam toward it, floating upwards in my crystalline water world, passing through a doorway of white silken veils into a circular room. Seated around the circumference of the room were many ancient women—

goddesses of every age from every culture. I knew I was welcome and, yet, the heat in the room was strong and their gaze so piercing, I wanted to flee. I imagined myself melting into the ocean floor, disappearing from their view and from my own inner eye.

Standing there, struggling to meet their collective gaze, shame washed over me, hot and red. I felt my skin prickle from the searing emotion, and I shifted uneasily. One of the goddesses rose, approached me, and asked, "What is it that you wish to hide?" Tears streamed down my face, sobs welled up from my belly and burst forth from my mouth. *"Shame!"* The word let loose a dam of pent-up feelings that were so intense, I could do nothing but sit on the crystal floor and weep. The women sat in silence until the tears ceased. The goddess who had spoken to me continued, "Thank you for your gift of trust," she said.

Slowly I floated from one woman to the next, reaching out to touch each one separately. I settled into the center of them, and one of the women spoke. "What is your one wish from us?"

"Teach me," I whispered.

A woman enveloped in shimmering silver robes moved gracefully toward me. In her outstretched hand she held a rose. She handed it to me and asked, "Where is the beauty in this rose?" I took the ruby red flower and stared at it. How could I possibly answer her question? The beauty seemed to be everywhere: in the color, the texture, the fragrance, the form. Each petal stood in its individual magnificence, shimmering with beauty and mystery.

Without speaking, the silvery woman took the rose from me, held it to her third eye, and then proceeded to pluck the petals and gently let them fall from her fingers, one by one, to the ground beneath my feet. She held the naked stem in her delicate hands, looked me in the eye and said, "Beauty is never in the manifestation of the physical. Rather it is born from the source that creates the physical. Beauty does not lie in its parts, but rather is a function of its totality. Essence creates beauty and not the other way around.

"What is the essence of this rose?" she asked me.

I answered her, from where I do not know. "The essence is spirit, the unknowable mystery from which life springs forth."

She nodded in agreement and asked, "Does that sometimes frighten you?"

I wondered how she knew. "Yes," I replied.

"You have nothing to fear from the unknown. It is full of challenge, mystery, and excitement. What frightens you is letting go of what you think you know. But what has the known ever given you?"

Nothing that I could think of. I didn't need to speak; she knew my thoughts. I listened to her instead. "Essence is a part of the unknowable, the things in life that we cannot explain. The unknowable is Great Spirit. You can experience it, but you will never know it. The unknowable is not to be feared; it is your own essence."

I bowed my head in gratitude. At that moment, a drum was placed in my hands. The ancient women in the circle played their golden drums that were connected to the prismatic lights reflected in the crystals. I drummed with them, joining my cadence with that of the women, as a great rainbow bridge was fashioned from my shaman center out into the universe. I moved my spirit out along the rainbow toward the stars. The more I drummed, the stronger and more distinct the rainbow grew.

A whistling elk made of blue and gold light approached me; she was carrying a lightning bolt in her mouth. I knew it was Agnes in her purest spirit form, meeting mine. In my inner voice, I gave thanks to the spirit of the elk that we might be able to create drums from her skins. I took the lightning bolt from her mouth and threw it far out into the universe. The elk spoke to me, telling me of the powers of the drum to bridge the worlds and to heal.

The elk began to slowly dissolve before my eyes, as I briefly lost consciousness. I stirred back in my body, numb and stiff, leaden with my full weight solid on the thinly carpeted floor. I cringed as each vertebra cracked and stung with the slightest movement. My life force was back in its protective shell, but something in me had changed. I had accepted beauty in its truth and purity; it had been redefined, and I was freed from yet another stereotypical idea of women and power. I would no longer see beauty as a tangible thing but rather as movement, as the flow of nature, ever-changing and transforming everything that it touched. As the silver goddess had told me, beauty was essence. Nothing more, nothing less.

Amid various group meditations, the next two days were spent in decorating our drums which were to be completed in time for the blessing of the drums ceremony on Saturday night. When I studied the outline of the elk hide I had stretched into a circle, I perceived a shape that reminded me of a butterfly in transition from the world of spirit into the world of form. I painted the images that were already there in soft greens and yellows. My decoration was complete. During the dreamtime meditation, I had received a name for my drum. I called it "Namasté," a Tibetan word meaning "The God in me greets the God in you."

With the passing of each day, I felt stronger and healthier and more vital. With Susie's help, caring for Gregory was effortless, and I felt truly supported for the first time since he was born. On Saturday night, we made a sacred fire in the center of a clearing. We all sat in a huge circle around the fire and burned juniper, a sacred herb for invoking and listening. Lynn directed us in our prayers and blessings. "In the smoke of this wild juniper, listen well. Agnes Whistling Elk and all of the women from the Sisterhood of the Shields are present for this ceremony, guiding us and showing us the deeper parts of ourselves. Know that Agnes is here in spirit, and you will be able to divine your individual messages from her in the next few minutes."

The smoke swirled around me like a protective cloak. I felt blessed by the presence of the women, and I felt that Agnes herself was infusing energy into me, filling up all the holes. When I awakened on Sunday morning, I knew that the medicine had worked. I would come away from this gathering with a new, more powerful sense of myself. We began our closing ceremony outdoors beside the meeting room, where all the women were gathered to beat their new shamanic drums. I held Gregory in my arms and swayed to the rhythm, which grew so powerful, I felt the earth beneath my feet reverberating each time the drums were struck.

Gregory, who had been calm and quiet all weekend, suddenly opened his mouth, and long, piercing bird sounds poured out of him. He was calling out to the women, answering their drumbeats. He continued serenading the women, his voice clearly distinguishable above the great booming sounds of the drums. All at once as if they were one person, the women stopped drumming and spontaneously turning to face Gregory, began calling back to him in parrot voices.

Joy and awe lit up my son's face. I was elated, and knew that changing medicine directions for the coming year was right. I was shifting from the south, trust and innocence, into the north, the place of challenges and the endurance to meet them. Before the completion of the gathering, when I took my turn to approach Lynn to receive a written message from Agnes, my spirit was awake, alive, and brilliant. For a moment I knew that I was shining like a star.

# 17

## LIVING THE GODDESS?

I MADE THE TRIP TO LOS ANGELES WITH GREGORY AND Susie, my standard entourage since the medicine gathering. This time we flew, and we arrived at Lynn's house slightly disheveled and wrinkled from the flight. After settling the other two in the outer office, I went into the living room to greet Lynn. The medicine gathering had been only two weeks prior, and we hugged with a sense of familiarity.

Lynn saged my body using an eagle wing, appropriate to my new power animal. I hadn't told her about the change, and I wondered how she knew. I breathed in the sage and realized how much more comfortable I felt in my own skin than the last time I had been here. We took our seats and, as usual, she devastated me with her first question. "How is your marriage?" she asked.

I opened my mouth to give her my pat answer, "Fine," but the word stuck in my throat. My face began to heat up, and tears prickled the corners of my eyes. I was embarrassed and frightened by my reaction; I seemed to have no control over myself. I wanted to be composed, I wanted her to see that I had changed, that I had finally become a woman of the north, filled with strength and wisdom. Instead, I just sat there, worn out, shaky, and on the verge of tears.

"You look sad," she said with kindness in her voice.

I sighed. "It's just that I don't know if it's me, or the relationship, or my fear of intimacy—or if it's Richard. I don't like the way he talks to me."

"How does he talk to you?"

"From his mind. He's intellectual. I feel like he's being condescending with me, and I don't like it." My speech was stilted, and I choked back my tears. I didn't want to talk about my marriage because I feared what Lynn might show me about myself. I tried to relax my hands, which were gripping the edge of the sofa.

"I see," Lynn said quietly. "But you have the wisdom," she added. Her eyes were looking to my left side, unfocused and unwavering. She was obviously seeing on a different level. She continued speaking. "His condescension drains your energy. You are so much in your feminine shield right now since you've had your child. You need to balance your energy." She relaxed back in her chair.

"It's like this: In life there is energy that swirls around." She made a swirling gesture with her hands. "It's filled with male and female energy. The male energy explodes, and the female energy implodes. It is essential that these forces be balanced. You have too much imploding energy. Do you understand?"

"Yes, I do." I hadn't been able to describe it, but recently I had had sensations that something was pressing on my chest and stomach from the inside, especially when Richard and I were arguing.

"I want you to shift these currents," Lynn told me. "What do you do when you fight with your husband?"

I flashed back to a few days earlier. Richard and I were lying in bed before going to sleep, and I got up to open the window.

"I don't want that window open," he had said forcefully. "The night noises will keep me awake, and I need my sleep."

"But it's so stuffy in here, *I* can't sleep! I'm usually happy to accommodate you, honey, but I feel closed in tonight. I'd like to keep it open for a little while."

"Jennifer, I'm sick of you imposing your will on me."

"Well, I'm sick of you being controlling."

Refusing to listen to me anymore, Richard had begun his onslaught about how selfish and thoughtless I was. I curled up into a ball, put a pillow over my head, and tried to shut him out completely. "I can't hear you, I can't hear you." I repeated this sentence over and over until he stopped talking.

As I pictured myself lying there curled up in a tiny ball, I looked like a five-year-old child, helpless to communicate, hiding from my aggressor. I wondered if Lynn had been reading the pictures in my mind. "If I'm lying down," I told her, "I curl up into a ball. If I'm sitting, I tuck my legs underneath me."

Lynn was sitting comfortably with her legs folded beneath her, holding a presence of self-assurance and relaxation. When I took the same position, my legs held self-consciousness and tension. Lynn studied my body with the faraway look that had become so familiar to me. "It's as if Richard has cut your legs out from under you. You should be very careful right now. You could easily fall and hurt yourself. When you leave my house, hold onto the handrail as you go down the stairs."

I looked at her, incredulous.

"I mean it!" she said with command in her voice. "You are vulnerable to injury. He's cut your legs off, and you have nothing to stand on."

The image of me having no legs was terrifying. I shifted my body and wanted to disappear into the corner of the couch. "Is that why I keep bruising my legs so much?" I asked her.

She nodded. A gentle summer breeze wafted through the open French doors and blew through me, dissolving my defensiveness. Defining what was wrong offered me a sense of relief. What did it matter how I looked to her or to anyone else? I just wanted to feel better, and I wanted to tell her everything. "When I try to talk to him about anything that's bothering me," I said, "he tells me it's my fault. Sometimes he says it's all in my imagination, and he just dismisses me."

"What do you do?" she asked.

"I start doubting myself, and then he tells me I have a problem. He says I should get help with my anger."

Lynn's eyes lit up. "It's time to start fighting fire with fire," she said. "You need to get more aggressive."

"But he's so good with words. He makes his side of it sound so logical, I can't catch his distortions. He says it's all about me, I get furious, and then I end up looking foolish."

"He has knowledge, Jennifer, but you have wisdom. Women have to take up the goddess in their lives and show men how to live. When you fight with Richard, I want you to change your body position."

"What do you mean?"

"I want you to stand up. I mean physically."

I wasn't sure I understood what she was saying. "Stand up on my feet?"

"Yes. Whenever you're arguing."

It had never occurred to me to stand up. How strange that would be! I already felt silly enough when we were fighting. Now she expected me to jump up out of bed in the middle of an argument and stand there. It felt completely foreign.

"I want you to stand up on your own two feet," she repeated, "and while you're standing there, I want you to imagine you just won the Nobel peace prize! Do you get it?" Lynn's body posture and voice reflected exactly what she was suggesting for me.

I was a little bit dubious, but I thought about it. Richard didn't have to know that I was thinking I had just won a prize. Maybe I could do it. It was certainly worth a try.

"You're afraid you're disposable to Richard," she told me. "There's a bully in him. But you can handle it, Jennifer. I know you can. The nature of the earth is feminine, so we women naturally understand the nature of things. Deep down, each woman knows that she knows. But we are taught that we don't know. For men, the energy of this planet is not familiar. So they don't know. But they are taught that they do."

"So it's all set up backward," I said.

Lynn smiled. "Yes, it is. We have to teach them. You have to teach Richard."

I knew Richard would never agree with her. I thought about "living the goddess." I liked the idea, but it also frightened me. I had heard about women over the centuries who had been punished and even burned at the stake for less. Although I had no idea what this meant in the twentieth century, I supposed it was different now. I imagined that Lynn wasn't referring to women dressing in long flowing gowns and going into trance. Rather, she was talking about women living up to their potential and taking a stand. There it was. Standing up instead of curling up into a ball and losing their legs to a man. I would do it.

I left Lynn's house still wondering if I'd feel silly standing up and arguing, but I would take up the staff of authority anyway and take a stand in my marriage. I'd try it the very next time we had a fight. I knew I wouldn't have to wait very long.

# 18

## TRANSLATIONS

DESPITE MY MISGIVINGS, I FOLLOWED LYNN'S instructions carefully. Whenever Richard and I were in a discussion and I started folding in on myself, I stood up. The minute I was on my feet, my entire perception changed, of him, of myself, and of the situation at hand. Whether I was seeing a client, walking the baby, or talking with my husband, I reminded myself that I had just won the Nobel peace prize. My rational mind kept reminding me that I hadn't, but I remained steady in my vision, which was often humorous to me. This added a lightness to the feeling of accomplishment and power I was building around my navel.

During my walks with Gregory, I spoke words of power that I had received in a meditation with Lynn. I chanted them over and over, willing them into my body and my mind. I spoke with an aggressiveness that was uncharacteristically fierce for me, and I felt these sacred sounds balancing my feminine and masculine energies.

The image of being a Nobel prize winner, combined with standing my ground, began to create subtle changes in my world, both inside and out. I was gaining the courage to say what I felt, and I no longer collapsed emotionally. I was surprised to find that an intense anger was replacing my previous weakness. Richard was dismayed when I stomped around in our heated moments. He hated the changes in me, he must have feared them, and since he had no idea what had brought them about, he had no idea how to counteract them. While I was taking a stand, he was losing ground. I was beginning to understand what living the goddess meant and, as foreign as it was, I liked it.

Lynn chuckled on the phone when I told her. "You're going to be a powerful woman when you resolve this," she said. "Do you understand that Richard is a mirror for you? You both must be getting something out of this for the dynamic to continue."

"I know," I sighed. "I've thought about it, but I don't know what it is."

"Do you know a good therapist who can help you?"

"Yes, yes. We're seeing one now." The weariness must have come through in my voice, because Lynn laughed again.

"I know it's frustrating, but you're gaining wisdom. I think you'll get exactly what you need from this, Jennifer, and you certainly want to do whatever you can to work it out because of the baby. But don't forget, you don't have to stay and be abused. It must be escalating because the changes in you are forcing Richard to change. He's been mirroring the part of you that is doubting and condescending."

"I know," I said in a half-whimper. "It's just that when we argue and he tells me it's my fault, I start wondering if he's right. Even when I'm standing up. It makes me feel like I'm crazy."

"Don't be down on yourself, honey. That dynamic would make anyone feel crazy. Maybe you ought to make an addiction doll for your addiction to being the problem. Remember, in order for women to teach men how to live, they have to learn to live the goddess."

"I'm doing what I can," I said, still not quite sure what living the goddess entailed.

"Before we hang up, I just want to tell you that Richard will probably get really angry before this is over. Expect it, and don't let it take you by surprise. Stay strong and ready."

I listened, but I only remembered Richard showing his anger once when I was pregnant and we were arguing about the nursery. Beyond that, he was always so contained, I had no idea what his real anger looked like. He rarely raised his voice above a scold, and it seemed that his favorite trick was to get me to raise *my* voice so he wouldn't have to be the one who did the yelling. The louder I got, the calmer he acted, as if yelling were beneath him. He kept his cool by provoking me into losing mine.

During this time, I started working with a new client. Janet was a beautiful, intelligent woman in her forties, who had postponed marriage and children for many years in favor of her career. She had finally married three years prior and had a baby boy who was several months older than Gregory. Janet's voice was soft, refined, and self-assured when she called to make her appointment.

During the introductory session, she told me that she was a high-ranking public relations executive with a major corporation in Silicon Valley. Her husband was a well-established physician who provided her with all the luxuries of life, but she wasn't happy. She got weepy as she described her relationship.

"It must be my intimacy issues. I don't like having sex with my husband anymore. Sometimes I get so mad at him for the way he talks to me, I just don't want to have anything to do with him."

"How does he talk to you?" I asked, feeling a sense of déjà-vu.

"He always thinks he's right. He lives in his mind, and he doesn't care about my feelings."

I nodded sympathetically. The similarities in our lives were stunning, and I could speak from experience. "When men and women meet, their instinctual selves are awakened. They make love, which shoots them up into spirit for a brief time. But soon, in the process of dealing with everyday life, men retreat into their minds and women retreat into their feelings. What you get are conversations that go like this: This is what I think about what you feel, and this is what I feel about what you think. Sound familiar?"

She gave a little laugh. "Yeah, that's exactly what happens."

"Unfortunately, these opposite styles don't lead to harmony, as you may have noticed."

"That's an understatement," she agreed. Her body had become slumped over in her chair, and she looked defeated. I knew just what to say next.

"What do you do when you argue with Arnold?" I asked her.

She looked surprised at my question. "Well, I guess I give up. I get so angry that he won't respect my feelings. And then I cave in." She thought a moment and became more animated. "A lot of the time, I can see his point of view. I understand his thinking. But for Arnold, his opinion is all there is. He won't even listen to my side of the story, and I end up feeling discounted and ashamed."

"What's the shame about?"

"He tells me he won't bother listening because I'm not smart enough. Then I'm afraid to talk at all because I don't want to sound stupid. He always seems so sure of what he's saying."

"Is it hard for you to stand in your truth?" I asked her.

"Yes," she said. "I leave the room and sink into a depression. I feel so hopeless. I just don't think he'll ever see my point of view. That's all I want. I don't even care if he agrees with me. I just want him to hear me."

I heard Lynn talking to me. "Take a stand. Take a stand," she repeated in my mind. "Janet, what are the qualities you associate with the truth?"

"When I think about truth, I feel relaxed and alive, or

maybe I should say energetic. For me, the truth feels buoyant and safe, even when it's painful."

I smiled broadly. "What a beautiful description! You have a good knowledge of the truth. That doesn't sound stupid to me. I want you to start noticing your interactions with yourself and other people. Notice when the truth is around. When you're talking to yourself or listening to other people, are you feeling alive or dead? For now, just experiment and play with it. Okay?"

"Okay," she said.

Several weeks later, Janet and her husband arrived for a couple's session. Arnold appeared pleasant and gracious as they walked in and sat down. He began speaking. "Janet wanted me to come along. She's been enjoying her work with you, and she thought it might be good for our relationship."

His voice was clear, his speech was articulate, and he was letting me know in no uncertain terms that he was not here out of personal choice. I wasn't sure which direction to take it from there, so I paused a moment to get my bearings. I decided to let them decide.

"So," I said. "Where shall we begin?"

Again, Arnold responded. "Janet and I have a serious problem with communication." He leaned forward, engaging me and excluding his wife as if she were not even in the room. "I love my wife, but we have a hard time meshing values. We can't seem to agree on much of anything." His voice had taken on a patronizing tone, as if he were speaking to the principal about his little girl who was having a bad time adjusting to school.

"Janet," I said, bringing her into the discussion, "how are you feeling right now?"

"I'm feeling small," she said in a barely audible voice.

"I want you to shift your energy." I directed her loudly. "I want you to feel big. *Big!* Think about these words: *strong, aware, self-confident, knowledgeable.*" I was speaking with intensity, trying to penetrate her shell of fear and weakness. I turned my attention back to Arnold. "You mentioned you had a communication problem," I said, "but I find you speaking very clearly. Where is the problem?"

Arnold blurted out, "It's Janet! She just won't agree with me."

"It's scary when people won't agree with you, isn't it?" I asked him.

"They might hurt me," he said, slumping over in his chair just the way Janet had done a few moments before.

"I understand. I see you've been very frightened. It must be exhausting for you to make sure everyone always agrees with you. But now I want you to try living beyond your fear. See if you can feel safe with Janet. You can keep up your debates with other people for now, until you've established a degree of safety with your wife."

I was surprised by the relief on Arnold's face. I wondered if anyone had ever acknowledged his fear and addressed it directly. I wondered if he had ever been safe enough to admit to having it. "Do you both want to come back next week?" I asked them.

In keeping with the pattern, Arnold spoke right up. "I want to try practicing on my own. I don't really need therapy."

I was hesitant to just let him go, but I had to let him do as he chose. "Old fear that has been with us for a long time generally has deeper roots than we imagine. You'd be surprised how much of our behavior happens according to past occurrences that we're not in touch with. It can be helpful to understand the origins of our fear, so if you get stuck, please call me."

"If I have any problems, I'll come back," Arnold assured me.

Janet said very little aside from murmuring a quiet good-bye, telling me she'd be calling.

Several weeks later, Janet called, and we spoke briefly over the phone. I wasn't at all surprised to hear that she and Arnold had had a terrible fight and wanted to schedule an appointment. They came in together the next day, obviously in the middle of an ongoing argument.

"Whoa, let's take a time-out here," I suggested. Janet and Arnold were sitting in front of me in the throes of a shouting match. They both looked startled and went silent. They weren't accustomed to a third party interrupting their all-too-familiar fights. "This can't only be about today. With this much friction between the two of you, there must be a hook here into some past issues, probably on both sides. I want each of you to talk about the past and how it connects to the present."

Arnold jumped right in. "She's just like my father. I could never please him, no matter what I did. He was irrational, and he was always mad at me."

"I'm not his father," Janet countered.

"No, you're not," I assured her. "This is Arnold's issue, and it isn't about you. He would have these feelings with anyone."

"But he keeps telling me I'm like his father."

I put my hand on Janet's shoulder to calm her. "You're not like his father. Take my word for it." She relaxed back into her chair.

Arnold smiled coyly. "She may not be exactly like my father, but she's emotional like my father."

"What does that bring up for you, Janet?" I asked her.

"My mother. She used to bellow at me just like Arnold does. My mother's hair was wild. She always looked disheveled and scary, and she obsessed about me being outside when it was dark. One morning, she started ranting that I'd been out in the middle of the night, and then she said I had to go to bed without dinner. I hadn't even had lunch yet. I was very young, maybe four or five, and I remember thinking, 'I can see the sun and it feels warm on my skin, but Mom says it's the middle of the night. How can that be?' I was completely disoriented, and I couldn't understand what my mother was telling me. I went to bed at noon."

"What does this have to do with me?" Arnold piped up.

"When you won't listen to my reality and say that yours is the only right one, it reminds me of my mother."

I interceded. "I'm surprised at both of you. You've said hurtful things to one another today. Your personal histories each have been filled with so much pain, you should be going out of your way to be gentle with each other. Haven't you been hurt enough?"

They looked at each other.

"So what's it going to be?" I asked them. "Are you going to keep on hurting yourselves, or do you want to heal your relationship? It's your choice."

They put their arms out and embraced each other. Janet cried, and Arnold held her. They had made their choice. We finished the session by discussing new ways of reacting and being more loving. When they left, I had a slight twinge of envy. I wanted a healing for my relationship with Richard, and seeing them walk out hand in hand with a new understanding made me wonder if I could do as much for myself.

# 19

## SACRED SOUNDS

M Y SISTER, SUSIE, WAS MARRIED IN AN ELEGANT country club in the town where we lived. The ceremony and the reception were elaborate; the food was abundant and the wine flowed. Her new husband was a good man, and they were happy together. I was glad for Susie. We had become closer since she had helped me out with Gregory, and I wanted her marriage to be successful. She and her husband left on their honeymoon with good feelings all around.

The next day my father fell ill. He complained that his body ached, and he wheezed and felt exhausted. He attributed it to the wedding festivities as he had drunk more than usual and thought he must have a very bad hangover. With a house full of guests, he knew he had to play host during the day after the big event, so he made everybody some gin fizzes, just to get going. They didn't perk him up the way he had hoped, so when all the wedding guests finally left, he went to bed.

The wheezing got worse, and he made an appointment with his allergist for the same day, fearful that his asthma was creating new problems. The allergist examined him thoroughly and, finding a heart murmur, sent my father to see a cardiologist. He went reluctantly, certain that they were making a big fuss about nothing. There they discovered that one of his heart valves had partially disintegrated; he was in congestive heart failure. He was admitted to the hospital the same afternoon.

I walked through the hospital halls, amazed at how quickly things happened. I stopped before I entered his room; I was afraid to see my father. What if he looked weak and feeble? How could I bear it? I took deep breaths and practiced the words of power I had learned in my group work with Lynn.

I knew that in Tibet, healers give people certain spiritual images called mandalas on which to meditate. The underlying principle is that viewing these particular spiritual images adjusts the vibrational frequencies of your body and your mind so that they will no longer be conducive to disease. Many healings had been reported through the use of these techniques and I supposed that repeating the words of power acted on similar principles: the harmonics of these words could shift negativity out of the central nervous system. Lynn never explained this outright; she always waited for her apprentices to experience things directly before she talked about them. But it felt logical to me that the principles overlapped.

The sacred words had come to me quite easily. In her last workshop, Lynn had invited us to go into the silence. "Move into the center of your inner universe. From this place, I want each of you to call forth your own individual words, which will act as your guiding sacred sounds.

The words will be different for each of you, and they are sacred to you. They are yours and yours alone. When you receive them, use them in difficult situations. They will help to calm and sustain you."

The sounds had floated to me as if they were riding on a light breeze: one word for protection, one for love, and another for power. When I spoke them, I could feel an altering in my vibrational frequency. I used these words now as I approached one of the most difficult things I would ever do: being with my father in his time of need. When I was ready to enter the room, I felt a calmness and great love for him.

The bed was empty, and at first sight, I had a rush of fear. Unfounded. My father was standing at the window, talking on the phone to a business associate in his clear, professional voice. I was relieved to see him upright, to hear his voice sounding normal and to see that he looked pretty well, just a little paler than usual. He smiled when he noticed me and gestured for me to sit in the chair. I gazed out the window, seeing nothing, while he finished his conversation. I continued to recite my silent words of power, and I felt centered, prepared to focus on his needs. Usually, I felt so overwhelmed by my father, I could barely listen to anything he said, but by the time he put down the phone, I felt courageous and relaxed. I had calmed down enough to listen to the story of his illness and the tests he was taking.

After spending about an hour with him, I gave him a book and a magazine I had brought, promising to return. I was grateful for my shamanic work; it had given me the tools to keep my heart open in a crisis. With my own father! We had managed to comfort each other, a far cry from the upset that we had sometimes caused each other in the past.

The tests went on. Sonograms, angiograms, blood work. There were meetings with the cardiologist, the surgeon, the anesthesiologist. The more tests they ran, the more problems they uncovered. The angiogram revealed not only the deteriorating valve, but also an occluded artery. That meant that in addition to valve repair, they also would have to do a bypass. X rays showed a spot on the lungs, and they were worried about cancer. At the very least, one operation was unavoidable. The date was set for immediately after Labor Day.

Each time I visited my father in the weeks prior to the surgery, I silently repeated my sacred words of power and was able to stay calm in the face of each new finding, each new danger, each new fear. Best of all, I could feel my father drawing comfort from my presence. He began speaking openly to me for the first time. I did the same with him; we discussed real and heartfelt issues. The inevitable stresses and tensions were there, but they were accompanied by truth and intimacy.

We each talked honestly about our life struggles in a tender and often humorous way. We understood each other's suffering, and we laughed together, delighting in the camaraderie. When I left his room, our good-byes were warm and compassionate. I cried tears of both grief and joy while something was happening that I had never thought possible: I was making peace with my father.

# 20

# RAINBOW MOTHER

JULIA, A TALL, GENTLE YOUNG WOMAN, REGAL IN STATURE, had been raised in an affluent, competitive environment. Her father, a property developer, had amassed a small fortune during the real estate boom in California. Her mother, an English aristocrat, had been raised by servants and had lived all over the world. A new client, Julia reclined easily in the forest green chair, which picked up the green flecks in her blue eyes. She was a beautiful woman with a powerful mind.

"What's wrong with this picture?" I asked myself, as I studied the inward pull of her shoulders and the deliberate casualness of her carefully crossed ankles. On first appearances, Julia had seemed touched by the gods with a kind of brilliance. But on closer scrutiny of her eyes and her body language, she was almost too much at ease, exhibiting a myriad of social skills that clearly had been developed to mask her underlying anxieties. Tension fluttered beneath her meticulously made-up eyes, her speech had a breathless quality, and her hands darted nervously as she spoke.

It took quite a few meetings before Julia opened up

about her family environment. Although her family had been loving and supportive, she felt terribly restrained within its social conventions and tedious routines. She wanted to be free and creative; she wanted her life to be spontaneous. At the same time, she didn't want to act in ways that would cause her family to reject her. She didn't want to make them into monsters in her mind, but she felt claustrophobic and trapped within values that were not her own. She yearned for adventure, to do things that would not fit within the strict conventional codes to which she was accustomed. She also didn't want to rock the boat or hurt anyone. Her biggest fear was to be considered an outsider by the people she loved the most.

I was hesitant to discuss shamanism with Julia, afraid it would sound strange to her and maybe even scare her away. Yet, I knew she needed it; there was a reason she had come to me and not some other, more traditional, therapist. I decided to approach the issue anthropologically.

"Have you ever heard of native cultures that honor the feminine or motherly qualities of receptivity, regeneration, connectedness, and community?" I asked her one day.

She stiffened perceptibly. A mask of quiet reserve covered her finely chiseled face. "I'm not sure what you mean," she said.

I was afraid that I had gone too far, that I had shaken our therapeutic relationship, but it was already done. I decided to press on. "In these ancient cultures, they identify two distinct types of female energy. I'm going to tell you a story of how my teacher explained these ancient teachings to me."

The idea of a story seemed to relax Julia. While I spoke, I concentrated my inner eye on a vision of Lynn, her long blond curls framing her face as she described these motherly energies. "Julia, first there is the nurturing mother, the bulwark of our social life. With her faculty for routine and her ability to create substance and form, she nurtures life and the children. She is known as Corn Mother, suckling babies and life itself at her breast.

"The other feminine energy is called Rainbow Mother. She is ecstatic and inspires people. She is the artist, the poet, and she does not fit into conventional life. When she tries and fails, she may turn to drugs or alcohol and become depressed."

Julia listened with great interest as I continued. "When my teacher asked me which one I thought I was, I told her I was definitely a Rainbow Mother. She disagreed, telling me she thought I was a Corn Mother trying to live the life of a Rainbow Mother in order to be like my own mother. I stubbornly held onto my point of view, trying to convince her with stories of how I danced, played music, and wrote in school. But as always, Lynn held firm by saying nothing."

"Why didn't you agree with her?"

"In my mind, a Corn Mother was burdened with unremitting drudgery that went unrewarded and unappreciated. Like Cinderella. I didn't want to be used, and I wanted to be seen; I wanted to have an exotic and fun-filled life. I wanted to be a free spirit. Although this was at odds with my desire for a committed relationship and a family, I couldn't come to terms with it.

"One year later, in a meditation at a medicine gathering, I had a vision of myself and knew for sure that I was a nurturer, a Corn Mother, but it wasn't the way I had imagined it. I saw the beauty of nurturing; I realized that there was magic in it. I was relieved and I wept for all the time I had been separated from myself. I don't know all the specifics of the Corn Mother's true nature—I'm still exploring that—but at least I know who I am."

"How did you find out more about it?" Julia asked.

"I study shamanism; I revel in my love of the earth, my life, and my dreams. I explore other levels of consciousness. I embrace the mystery of the universe, and through that, I learn about myself."

I sat back and paused. I had taken a risk by sharing myself beyond the therapeutic confines, but I felt strongly that it was the only way to show Julia how to heal. She was leading a fully functional life, but she was devoid of spirit. How could she possibly be fulfilled?

"So, which energy are you?" I asked her.

She answered quickly. "I must be the nurturing energy, the Corn Mother."

"You've certainly been living that way," I agreed, "but has it satisfied you?"

"No. I want more," she said definitively. The intensity of her own words startled her. She had spoken with such clarity, she almost sounded angry.

"Maybe the 'more' you're seeking is the rainbow energy."

Her eyes clouded over, and her face flushed. "When

you say that, it feels right in my heart," she whispered, as if afraid to acknowledge her own understanding. "But it doesn't fit in with the rest of my life."

"Why don't you start exploring it privately and see what happens. It may be different than you think."

She agreed. In the weeks to come, Julia and I practiced meditation together. I taught her to find her sacred words of power that would help her to make changes in her inner world. She continued to have sessions with me, and as she integrated the new rainbow characteristics and qualities into her lifestyle, she began to feel more comfortable.

"How are you doing?" I asked Julia one afternoon.

"Very well," she said. "The most important thing that's happening is my relationship with my family. I thought that if I went along my own path, it would separate me from them, but the opposite has happened. The more fulfilled I feel as a person, the more I can be free to love them."

Julia and I sat in silence, allowing the sacred dreamtime to fill the space between us. I felt happy both for her and for myself. While she was getting the healing she had asked for, I was realizing my greatest dream: to incorporate my shamanic work with the therapeutic process in a way that would enhance both worlds. I knew it was only the beginning.

# 21

# THE HELP OF UNSEEN HANDS

WHILE MY FATHER SLOWLY RECOVERED FROM open heart surgery, the fall of that year marked the beginning of my personal unraveling. It all started with a shift in my workplace. The office building in which Richard and I rented work space was sold, and the new landlord was raising the rent so high, we had to leave. I hadn't been using my office as much since Gregory's birth, so it wasn't such a big issue for me. I could easily find another place to work, but for Richard, it meant a huge shift.

He acted unfazed. He said he actually was relieved, that he hadn't really liked that office building anyway. Over the last few years, he had put aside a nest egg of money for just such an occasion. He called it his "Fuck you" money, and it would allow him to walk away from his present circumstances at any time. After he moved, he planned to start a consulting business on predicting violent behavior in the workplace. He was certain it would be successful.

With these plans in mind, we both needed to find new office space. Around this time, I was asked to give two separate talks. One would be about the ethics of dual relationships with clients, a situation where a therapist has both a professional and private relationship with a client. When a therapist uses a client's emotional vulnerability to serve his or her own needs, it is considered abuse, a gross misconduct, and I was eager to speak about it. The second talk would be about recovery from chemical dependency, another topic with which I had experience and felt passionate about. I said yes to both; I needed to rebuild my client base, and giving talks was the perfect way to accomplish this. The scheduled dates for both talks were during the week before I was to do a seminar on shamanic mask making. It was a lot of work jammed into a small amount of time. The pressure cooker was on, and something had to give.

I did my work and I enjoyed it, but I was weary. Richard was taking apart his business, and I had to do the majority of the household chores during this busy time. I was being housekeeper, mother, therapist, teacher, shaman, speaker, daughter, and wife. I could barely keep it all together, and Richard agreed that I should hire someone to do the housecleaning for the month. I called and made the arrangements, relieved that a friend's maid would be free to help out.

"How often do you intend to have her come?" Richard asked in a disgruntled voice when I told him the plans were in place.

"Look," I said. "We talked about this last week, and you agreed. If you had a problem, you should have mentioned it then. I've already made the arrangements."

"But I didn't know last week how I'd feel today."

"We went over this in therapy, and you told Larry I was doing too much. You agreed that getting a cleaning lady would help me to ease the tension. I'm paying for it with my personal savings."

"Jennifer, I have the right not to want a stranger cleaning my house."

I threw my arms up in the air. Stomping upstairs, I fell into bed and stared at the ceiling. I felt unseen and unloved. Richard obviously didn't care about me. All he cared about was justifying his position. It had taken me all this time to get it. He didn't really care about me emotionally; he just needed what I could provide for him, and one of those things was someone to push around and fight with. I felt poisoned and sick to my stomach. I was not interested in having any more useless discussions with him. From now on, I would act as if I were single. He would be my roommate, nothing more.

I ignored him when he came to bed, but I was restless and couldn't sleep. I tried breathing exercises to relax; I envisioned Lynn and Agnes and the Sisterhood of the Shields. Nothing worked. I felt uncomfortable lying there in the dark with Richard, so I got up and turned on the hall light. I got back in bed and dozed fitfully until after one o'clock, when Gregory awoke for his feeding. Twenty minutes later, Gregory was sound asleep again, and I was wide awake. I sat up and began writing in my journal.

Richard stirred in the bed beside me. "What's wrong with you Jennifer? You seem so agitated," he said.

I knew he was provoking me into talking, and it could

only end in trouble, but I took the bait anyway. "I *am* agitated," I told him.

"You really need to do something about your state of mind," he said condescendingly.

Rage exploded inside of me. I turned to him and said through clenched teeth, "Sometimes I get so mad at you, I'd like to kill you."

Richard sat up and began a drawn-out monologue describing me as a highly disturbed person who needed help. I screeched that I'd like to slit his throat. Richard launched into a dissertation on my pathology. I couldn't take it anymore. I interrupted him and said, "I may be crazy or disturbed or anything else you feel like saying, but I'd rather die than go on living like this."

Richard quieted down, grabbed a piece of paper from his bedside table, and wrote something down. He turned to me, his face seething with anger. "You can't threaten to kill me," he hissed. "I've just written down your threats, word for word, and this is the last night you'll spend in this house. I want you out of here in the morning. I'm getting a lawyer tomorrow, and I'm taking Gregory. You'll never see him again. You're an unfit mother!" I was amazed to see him in such a fit of rage. He was yelling, just as Lynn had predicted. "In fact," he bellowed, "I want you out of here now!"

It was 2:00 A.M. "I'm not going anywhere," I told him.

Richard stomped over to my side of the bed. "Get out!" he screamed, with his finger pointing at the door.

"No!" I screamed back.

He reached for my arm and dragged me out of bed

and across the floor. My back banged against the bed frame and the floorboards, but I felt no pain. I could think only of my son; I needed to stay here and protect him. Richard was pulling me toward the stairs, and I grabbed onto the door jamb with my feet. With a lurching movement, I wrenched free from his grasp and scrambled back to bed. He followed close behind me. He had completely lost his cool, his body was trembling, and his face was infused with blood.

"Get out!" he yelled. "You're going down those stairs if I have to throw you down."

I shook my head no, terrified of what he might do, but determined to stand my ground. Suddenly, he was dragging me across the floor again. He had hold of the same arm, which was aching terribly by now, and he was pulling me toward the edge of the stairs. I had visions of being hurled down the stairs, lying dead at the bottom with a snapped neck. My son! What would he do without me? I grabbed onto the bathroom door jamb with my free hand, and Richard set to work loosening my fingers. I wondered if he was about to kill me, right after I had said I wanted to kill him.

He managed to pry my fingers loose, and then he pinned me down with his body on the floor next to the bathroom. We were both breathing heavily as he paused to regain his momentum. Suddenly, we heard a distressed cry coming from Gregory's bedroom. His voice pierced through the hostile air, and then there was silence. "Get off me," I said.

Richard stood up. I walked into Gregory's room and

held him. He smiled and laughed, and the incongruity of it all made me laugh, too. I swayed on my feet, rocking my son back and forth. I felt that there was no more physical danger, but I worried about Richard's threat of taking Gregory from me. I considered sleeping with him downstairs in the living room. But no. This was my home, that was my bedroom, and I refused to be displaced in the middle of the night. I put Gregory in his bed and walked back to my room. Richard was sitting at the edge of our bed. His face was soaking wet—he must have splashed water on it—and his hair was dripping and rumpled. His eyes were hard and set, his mood sullen and downcast.

"You still look dangerous," I said.

"You bet I am," he muttered, reaching for the phone. In the next moment, I heard him telling the police that his wife had just threatened to kill him and would they please come and apprehend me. I was shocked and propelled into action. I slowly walked into Gregory's room while he was still on the phone and carried my son downstairs. Richard followed close behind, passed me in the hallway, and grabbed my car keys from the dish by the door. Feeling like a trapped animal, I paced back and forth, never letting go of Gregory. I looked over at the diaper bag and remembered that I kept a spare key in the side pocket.

Richard, satisfied that I wasn't going anywhere, got back on the phone with the police dispatcher, while I floated over to the diaper bag, moved toward the back door, and let myself out. With great focus, performing one task at a time, I carefully buckled Gregory into his car seat, got into the front seat, and placed the key in the ignition. The car turned over but wouldn't start. My heart jumped. Richard approached the car door. I locked all the doors at once and continued to tease the starter. Richard was trying to unlock my door, so I held down the lock with one hand while I turned the ignition key with the other. The engine kicked over. Richard backed away and raced toward the automatic garage door to close it. I threw the car into reverse and backed out within an inch of the closing door. It was split-second timing, like a *Die Hard* movie, but this was no fantasy. It was real life, and I was running for my life with my son.

I took a different route than usual, afraid that Richard would try following me. Carefully driving well below the speed limit, I made it to my father's house. I marveled at the dreamy quality life had taken on as I parked the car, unbuckled my son from his car seat, and walked into the safety of my father's house.

# 22

## TAKING A STAND

TWELVE WOMEN SAT IN A CIRCLE ON A THICK DARK blue mat in an old warehouse, passing the Kleenex box. Each woman took her turn telling her story of what had brought her to a self-defense class. I sat to the teacher's right and was the first to speak.

"Starting from when I was four and my sister was eight," I said, "my caretaker used to burst into our room in the middle of the night, swinging her arms around, breaking everything in sight. Her eyes would bulge as she grabbed coat hangers from the closet. She'd be ranting and swearing while she pulled down our pajama bottoms and beat us." I swallowed hard, detesting these memories. I blew my nose and continued. "We never knew what made her so mad, so we never knew when it would happen. The nighttime was always dangerous, and the mornings were painful. We had stinging welts all over our bodies, and then my sister had to go to school and I had to be with my caretaker, acting as if nothing had happened." I sat back to breathe, unable to say anything else.

"Thank you, Jennifer," our teacher Carolyn said, her

189

warm brown eyes looking kindly into my own. I passed the Kleenex box to the next speaker.

This was a class called Model Mugging, a unique self-defense course in which women practiced fighting with men who were dressed in protective padded suits. This training was based on the fact that women do not naturally fight back; we have been trained to be the peace-keepers. In order to defend ourselves successfully, we have to retrain our muscular responses at a cellular level to automatically defend ourselves. In Model Mugging, because we cannot see our mock attackers' faces and they are completely protected from head to toe, we can turn them into anyone we want and let out all our aggressions without hurting them. This was a way to learn to fight back when it was necessary.

The violence I had been subjected to in my past had left me with feelings of powerlessness. I needed to know not only that I could take care of myself but, even more important, that I deserved to be protected. Telling my story was cathartic; I needed to speak up and let other women know these awful secrets. But I still held onto secrets from the present. What I didn't say in the opening circle was that six weeks ago, my husband had attacked me physically, dragging me around and attempting to throw me down the stairs—and that I was still living with him.

I also didn't say that in response to Richard's calling the police, an officer had come to my parents' home, where I had stayed temporarily. He was there to evaluate my mental competence, but by the time we finished talking, he had asked me if I wanted to press charges against Richard. That was the last thing I wanted, but if I didn't charge him, I was afraid that he would try to take Gregory from me. The day after the assault, I went down to the police station and allowed a woman police officer to photograph my injuries. When she saw my arms and back, she raised the misdemeanor charges to a felony. The following day, a series of nasty black-and-blue marks showed up, running all the way down my left leg, so I returned and had her take some additional pictures.

Larry, our therapist, had suggested that I stay at my parents' home during this time, but he felt that the situation was healable. That was what I wanted to hear. In spite of being stiff, sore, and having terrible rug burns, I was still looking for a way to heal the relationship. I was afraid to tell these women that I had dropped the charges. I still struggled with memories of the fight, and I was afraid that I had somehow caused it. Had I provoked Richard's violence? If I had, what could I do to make amends?

Richard had admitted that I didn't deserve his attack, but he still accused me of being responsible for it. "Most men eventually will be violent with you Jennifer, because you are exceptionally difficult," he had told me. Rage had seared through me at his words, and yet I felt powerless to do anything about it. I couldn't stop the inner voices from saying to me, "Maybe it *was* your fault." I had collapsed inwardly, but I was here to change that. I was here to shift the childhood beating pattern. It was just too much to admit verbally, but I was determined that if Richard ever tried it again, I would be ready for him.

After we each had told our individual story, Carolyn rose to demonstrate that women have the physical abilities to defend themselves. Two monsterlike shapes shuffled into the room, creatures in suits that were padded from head to toe, complete with helmets and boots. They were a monstrous and foreboding sight to every woman in the room. They stood motionless beside Caroline, looking like twin Godzillas, while she explained to us the different parts of the body such as the knees and the genitals, which are the most vulnerable to attack. Then she motioned for one of the fearsome opponents to approach her.

I watched her place her hands in the air in front of her, palms facing forward in a gesture of no resistance. "Don't come any closer," she told her approaching mugger. When the mock assailant ignored her request and began to enter what was her personal space, she drew her arms more closely to her body and took one step back on her right foot. With her palms still facing forward, her right elbow dropped back and instantly shot forward. She connected with him squarely in the nose, marked by tape on his helmet. "It doesn't matter how strong you are," she told us. "Getting hit in the nose hurts the same if you're a one hundred–pound weakling or a two hundred eighty–pound hulk. Now I want you to notice what happens when I hit my assailant again in the nose."

She hit him in the nose once again, and the mugger's

head lurched backward. As Caroline stepped into the space between the two of them, I noticed that the force of his head being thrown back had caused his hips to thrust forward. Caroline brought her left knee sharply up into his groin. He doubled up, and his head was pitched forward involuntarily. He took a step to regain his balance while Caroline used her right knee to smash him in the head. I was aghast, my body trembling, nausea rising from the pit of my stomach to the back of my throat. Violence terrified me, and being so close to it was repulsive to my system. The mugger pulled off his helmet to show us that he was still in one piece, and the women in the room took a collective breath.

"We're getting ahead of ourselves here," Caroline said. "We're going to learn all of these techniques, but for now, let's begin at the beginning. In the majority of attacks on women, they initially get thrown to the ground, so that's what I want to concentrate on." I had a flashback of Richard pulling me from the bed to the floor. I felt the bile in my stomach rising as Caroline's voice was un-remitting in the background. I wondered if I could go on with the class. I felt that I couldn't cope. I thought of Gregory; he would be getting up from his nap about now. He probably needed to nurse. I wanted to leave, longing to be safe at home with his soft mouth at my breast.

Caroline and her mugger were demonstrating a ground attack. The monster walked up behind her, and placing both of his arms around her waist, he lifted her high into the air. Turning, he laid her down on the ground and lay down beside her. Caroline stopped in this vulnerable position to give us instructions. "See how his arms are around me? I can't move my arms at all, but I can bite." She leaned forward, and putting her mouth to her mugger's arm, yelled out the word "Bite!" She explained what she was doing. "In these classes, the one thing we actually can't do is bite. The protective suit is not made for this, and you could injure him. So replace the action by yelling. Is that clear?"

I nodded through a haze of terror and resistance, as did the other participants. Caroline and her cohort were relentless, continuing on with their demonstration. I couldn't understand how she could focus in the middle of such intensity. "Now that your arms are free, put your weight on them and use the leverage to swing your legs around with your knee bent in this position, like so." She brought her left knee up near her face. "Notice that I'm protecting my face with my knee, and I can pivot around on my hip." Lithely, she swung around as her attacker shifted positions.

She stopped dead and stared at all of us. "You have to go against your instincts and move into your assailant's space. I know you want to do the opposite, but you have to move in." She hitched herself forward and with the coiled strength of her upraised leg, she kicked the mugger in the face. He fell backward onto the mat with a resounding smack. Caroline walked away from him, leaving him lying on the ground. I still wanted to bolt, feed my son, do errands, argue with Richard, anything but face a confrontation with this fearsome monster in padded clothing.

"Okay, women. Divide yourselves into groups, and let's practice the leg strikes," Caroline directed.

We practiced for about forty-five minutes, and just when I felt I couldn't handle it any longer, Caroline announced that we were about to start practicing with the phantom. We lined up against the wall and one by one, each woman stepped out alone on the blue mat. Bait. An accident waiting to happen. The mugger ran up behind the first woman and threw her onto the floor. "Elbow! Bite! Kick!" Caroline yelled out instructions. Eventually the woman was successful in knocking out the mugger. Then it was on to the next woman.

My turn arrived. I stepped out on the blue mat, afraid for my life. I clenched my fists, and tears ran down my face. I was amazed at how gently the mugger threw me to the floor. I heard the screams of the other women, encouraging me to defend myself and fight for my space, such an alien concept until now. I breathed in deeply, gathered all of my strength, and threw my elbow into the mugger's stomach. I quickly rolled onto my side and hit him a glancing blow to the head. Not strong enough. I heard Caroline yell for me to move in closer to the monster. My mind was numb now, my body working independently as I cocked my leg back and hit the mugger squarely in the face. He fell back and did not get up. My classmates cheered. My legs were jelly beneath me as I returned to the line. Caroline threw me a smile, before she turned her attention to the next student.

By the end of the first class, we had learned how to defend ourselves from attacks from behind when we were thrown to the ground. We learned eye strikes, ground kicks, and knockout blows to the head. After five hours, I was worn out and wobbly in the legs, but I was empowered by the adrenaline and my new skills and knowledge. In one day, I had broken through the myth that women cannot take care of themselves.

During the week following, I was bombarded with images of violence that had occurred during my childhood. I allowed the images to play in my mind and mentally applied my new skills to them. I went through scenarios of how I might have handled things differently and how I certainly would handle things now if anyone ever threatened me again. As I resolved my past fears, I felt new energy flooding through me.

Lynn had spoken repeatedly of the importance of women "finding our voices" and "owning our power." She had suggested we find ways to practice these things. Model Mugging was such a task, definitely in keeping with my new position of the north, the place of personal power, endurance, strength, and wisdom. It was time to take up my power and live my life beyond my negative childhood conditioning.

In the second class, we learned how to defend ourselves while we were standing up. We also covered special techniques for sexual assaults, particularly important for women who had been sexually abused either as helpless children or as adults. Our emotions were taxed while we exhausted ourselves practicing with each other and then, once again, went through being attacked by these strange beings who reminded me of the Mighty Morphin Power Rangers. This area of sexual abuse was so highly charged, the tension was far more intense than the previous week.

In the morning before the third class, Richard and I had a fight. When I felt it escalating, I told him that I didn't want to discuss it, but he kept right on talking. I had been up half the night with Gregory and spent the little energy I had left fighting with Richard. I arrived at class nearly an hour late, scattered and disoriented from lack of sleep, my eyes red from crying. But I was there. I knew that was what mattered.

The theme of the day was boundaries. When Carolyn saw the state I was in, she encouraged me to speak. Until that morning, I didn't know my fights were about inadequately defending my emotional boundaries, but when I paused to gather my thoughts, I was able to see things from a new point of view. I told the class how I had tried to set a boundary by telling Richard to leave me alone, and he had paid no attention. Again I had said, "Leave me alone!" and, again, he had pressed on with his argument. By the third time I told him to stop, I was yelling and had left myself wide open to his subtle manipulations. He had taken on a startled, abused look, and in his bland voice that so infuriated me, had said, "Jennifer, you really have a problem with anger."

The more I spoke with these empathetic women about my feelings of inadequacy to protect myself, the more support they showed me. They all understood; they were in the class also. I had nothing to feel ashamed about. I simply needed to tell the truth and then do something about it. My eyes filled with tears, and the tight band across my chest loosened. Perhaps I was not crazy. Maybe I wasn't the problem. When the class ended, Carolyn gave us a homework assignment to practice saying no at least once during the coming week.

"No problem," I thought to myself. "I can do that easily. After all, I'm a therapist and a shaman. And now I have formal training in self-defense. I'm assertive with my clients all the time. I can certainly say no in my personal life."

My opportunity arose when Richard and I were scheduled to interview potential baby-sitters for Gregory. Richard had set up a meeting with a Russian immigrant who was a classically trained pianist. He had met her through a neighbor and was excited by her talents, her warmth, and her strong emotional presence. He thought she would make a terrific sitter for Gregory. We had agreed that since the actual child care would take place in our home, we would conduct the interviews there. But Richard had arranged for us to interview this woman at a friend's house, where we also could listen to her play the piano. I wasn't pleased about this arrangement; the goal was to find a baby-sitter, and spending my Sunday at a piano recital of someone I didn't know was of little interest to me. I decided that this would be my "no" for the week. As diplomatically as I could, I told Richard how I felt and offered to make the call to reschedule the meeting at our house. He could listen to her play the piano some other time.

Two hours of intense dialogue ensued. Richard stood across the room from me with his hands in his pockets, pacing the white tiled entryway and analyzing my refusal to do as he asked. He said that he wanted to get to the bottom of it, to see what it really meant. He accused me of purposely being difficult and nonsupportive of him. I repeatedly held to my "no" as he tried every way he knew to get me to change my mind.

"Richard, please respect my preference in this," I said.

"I would, Jennifer, but I don't think it's in everybody's best interests, so how can I respect it in good conscience?"

"Because it's what I want, and interviewing her elsewhere goes against our original agreement. Remember we agreed that we would hold our interviews here so we could see how someone would fit in with our home and our lifestyle?"

"You have to learn to be flexible. I think you're sabotaging our chances to get the best sitter possible for our son. I've already arranged it, and she might feel badly if I cancel. Don't you see that we'll probably lose her because of your rigidity?"

In the end, I capitulated. I agreed to go and felt sick in my heart. I had failed in this simple homework assignment, proving to myself that I still couldn't stand my

ground with my husband, no matter that I was a therapist or a shaman or anything else. As we got into the car
to meet with her, I wondered how many times in our
marriage I had avoided saying no just to sidestep the
inevitable tirade that would follow. I was certain I must
have abandoned myself and my desires many times when
I didn't even know I was doing it. But now that I was
aware, it felt even worse.

We discussed the baby-sitter appointment with Larry.
After we had each thoroughly presented our sides and
our perceptions of the disagreement, Larry turned to
Richard with a puzzled look on his face. "So you were
willing to sacrifice your wife's preference and the harmony in your relationship for an appointment with a rel-
ative stranger?" he asked.

I was startled by the piercing quality of truth in his
words and the fact that he clearly wasn't labeling me the
problem. I had felt at the time that Richard was running
all over me. Larry's support had reaffirmed that I truly
hadn't wanted to sabotage anything; I simply wanted to
reschedule the appointment. I was even willing to make
all the arrangements. If it was such a huge problem for
this woman to change plans, maybe she wasn't the right
person after all. I gathered my strength and turned to
Richard to tell him how I felt. "I don't appreciate the way
you treated me," I said. My voice was clear and strong.

"It wouldn't have gotten out of control if you hadn't
been so difficult," he said, still clinging to his position.

I sat back and sighed with disgust. Even with Larry's
intervention, Richard was unwilling to budge. I won-

dered if there ever would be room for me to be my own person with him, separate from his needs and expectations. Ever since I began the Model Mugging class, more and more illusions about our relationship were being stripped away.

In the fourth class, Carolyn talked about commitment. She asked us if we were willing to make a commitment to finish a fight, no matter how tired, defeated, or sick we felt. I reviewed my past; during the last nineteen years, which I had devoted primarily to healing, the appropriateness of defending myself either physically or emotionally had never occurred to me. How had I missed that piece? Perhaps I hadn't missed it at all, but rather had made an unconscious decision that if I defended myself, I would be acting like my childhood perpetrator. I didn't want to see myself like that: ugly, violent, aggressive, or disrespectful. The thought of finishing a fight was alien to me, but I thought about how freeing it might be to commit myself to being my own bodyguard and no longer being swayed by what other people told me.

In our session that day, our muggers shouted out threatening verbal attacks as they attacked us physically. It was our job not to believe them. They yelled that I was about to die, that I deserved it because I was nothing and didn't matter to anyone. I held my ground. I could feel a detached presence growing within myself, and I knew that I didn't have to believe them or agree with anything they were shouting at me. Their words were just angry outbursts, and by taking action and fighting back, I not only was defending myself, but also proving them wrong.

Historically, I had believed that healing required softness. Most of my teachings had validated this belief. Now I could see that in some instances, growth required a strength and firmness that would not bend, an openness that would not turn away from the truth, no matter how painful it was. This was the day that I turned it around. I would apply this principle to my interactions with everyone, especially Richard. I no longer saw myself as the problem. In fact, I never had been the problem. There were things that I simply could not control, and as I accepted my grief about these things, I also could accept myself with compassion. I was back on the shamanic path with a brand new piece of the puzzle.

For our graduation class, fifty people, mostly strangers, were seated around the mats in the large vaulted space. In front of them, we practiced our new skills. I knew that Richard did not want to come, but when his brother, Steven, and his wife, Christie, accepted my invitation, Richard could hardly say no. They knew nothing about our fight, and Richard's absence would have been a bad show. The pressure was on.

It was difficult at first when I saw him in the audience, his face strained, his body visibly shut down. I had stage fright, but as it dissipated, something else kicked in. The word *"No!"* welled up and burst out of my mouth as I fought for my life. I was speaking to my husband, showing him that he no longer had physical power over me. Each time I threw one of my mock oppressors to the floor, another layer of old conditioning and fear sloughed off, leaving a new, shiny layer of personal power, ready to be utilized. With each blow, I was telling Richard in my mind, "Don't mess with me!" and I saw that new responses had been programmed deeply into my muscles. With my body and my voice working in harmony, I was no longer at odds; everything in me was protecting me and fighting for me.

When the demonstration was finished, we took time to talk with our guests. Christie rushed up to me while I was still out of breath. "Where do I sign up?" she asked, hugging me excitedly.

"What did you think?" I asked Steven.

"Boy, it was really exciting! To think that women can learn to take such good care of themselves and fight back if they need to." He put his arm around his wife. "I can't wait for Christie to learn these skills. And, Jennifer, you were great! I'm really proud of you." He gave me a big hug.

I turned to Richard. He was silent when he leaned forward to give me a mechanical peck on the cheek. He was holding himself rigid and looked like he'd rather be anywhere else. "What do you think?" I asked him.

"Frankly, it was difficult to watch. I'm not into violence, and it made me really uncomfortable."

I remembered how I felt in the first session; I could understand his discomfort, and I quietly nodded my acknowledgment. Over the next few weeks, my sense of helplessness continued to die away while a budding, quiet contemplative wholeness was emerging. I vowed to help it grow.

# 23

# LUCID DREAMING

I SPENT MY SATURDAYS RUNNING A FAMILY PROGRAM for a local chemical dependency hospital. The day ended with a group session comprised of patients, their spouses, and other family members.

One particular Saturday, I was struck by how all present seemed stuck in their heads as they tried to express themselves. I stopped the dialogue for a moment. "Everybody check in with your bodies for a minute," I directed them. It was clear from the looks on their faces that they were feeling disconnected. I encouraged them to talk about that, to speak their truth from their hearts and they would begin to feel better. A woman raised her hand. In a clear, emotional voice, she began to talk about the verbal abuse she had received from her husband. When she was finished, she said, "I didn't deserve this treatment. I don't deserve it now. I deserve respect."

"Yes, you do," I agreed.

Suddenly a man to my right named Howard piped in, "I don't think anyone *deserves* respect. I think people have to earn it." Several male voices mumbled in agreement as an uncomfortable wave passed over the room.

I turned to face Howard. "I would be interested to know how respect plays out in your life, Howard. Where do you have respect and where do you feel you don't have it?" There was an edge of sharpness in my voice. I wished my tone could have been more neutral.

Howard's face was getting redder by the moment. I could see his anger escalating, and I wondered if he was angry because a woman had said she deserved respect. He spoke through his rage. "I still think you have to earn respect, that nobody just deserves it."

I glanced at the woman who had been brave enough to begin this conversation. She was visibly wilting, the features in her face crumbling in defeat. My own anger surfaced as I faced Howard, but at the same time, I felt surprisingly focused and poised as I spoke. "This woman has looked inside herself and found that she is worthy of respect. She is not asking permission for it, and she is not inviting an argument or a philosophical debate. She made a statement about her self-knowledge. Now you might look inside yourself and find the same answer or a different one. I'd certainly like to hear how respect works in your life, but I'm not interested in hearing intellectualizations that take away from this woman's healthy self-acknowledgment."

"I don't know what you mean," Howard said, looking down into his lap and then glancing up at me.

I softened, feeling some compassion for him. He truly didn't know what I meant, and he had no idea how to communicate outside of his intellectual barriers. "Okay,"

I told him in a gentler voice. "It's something for you to think about."

The masculine aspect of my personality was healing, greatly accelerated by the self-defense classes. This healing also had begun showing up in my dreams. Male figures were appearing on a regular basis, and they had less and less desire to destroy, maim, or create chaos. They were clearly there to help me.

There was one male figure in particular, a warrior type with a chiseled face, who came to me when I was being accused of harming someone. In the dream, I felt powerless to stand up for myself, and accompanied by another weaker man, I was fleeing. My companion in flight was a sleazy character who knew I was innocent, and yet I didn't trust him. I knew that if it suited him, he would betray me.

My warrior arrived with intimate knowledge of my circumstances, and although he would not take care of me, his strength and firmness inspired me. I knew it was my job to handle the situation for myself and, in the light of his goodness and clarity about the truth, I felt comforted. Without the slightest doubt of my capabilities, he guided my companion and me into the wilderness and motioned for us to follow him on a 90 degree vertical climb up a mountainside.

I watched the individual muscles stand out on the warrior's back and arms as he masterfully propelled himself up the sheer incline. My sleazy companion did not have the strength it took to follow him with ease. He struggled hopelessly while the warrior confronted him on his lack of integrity in his dealings with me. He scraped and clutched at the ground while the warrior spoke to him about potential deceit and betrayal. Somehow, this weak man finally managed to scramble to safety at the top of the incline.

Now I panicked. It was my turn to climb the hill, and I strongly doubted my abilities to make it to the top. I placed one hand and one foot in front of the other and started climbing until, losing my grasp, I slid backward part of the way down the hill. The warrior reached out to me, not with his hands but with his intent and focus. His concentration was so great and affected me so profoundly, I gathered my scattered energies and climbed, finally reaching the top.

The warrior drew us deep into the woods and the further we walked, the more connected I felt to this powerful man. We entered a clearing and saw a large stone house with smoke curling from two separate fireplaces at each end of the dwelling. Instinctively, I knew that this was my warrior's home, and I felt privileged to be there. I knew that my unethical companion was about to accuse me falsely, that it couldn't be avoided as it was a necessary ordeal, but this stone house was a safe place to face his accusations. The warrior indicated that we would eat one last meal in preparation for the final fasting and cleansing. I knew that he would disappear while I prepared it, and when I watched him leave through the back door, I didn't want him to go.

In melancholy, I slowly began to prepare the food. My wimpy male companion stayed by my side, taunting and harassing me, telling me I'd be lucky if I ever saw the warrior again. Despondent at his words, I moved away from him and walked behind the house to shift my energy and lift my depression in the sweet scent of the woods. There I saw my warrior, involved in preparation tasks for our next level of cleansing. He noticed me and smiled. My heart lifted. He came to me and took my hand, inviting me to come and fast and dream with him. Hand in hand, we walked further into the dense woods, stopping at a cave that was being warmed by a fire. Sheepskin rugs covered the earth and healing herbs hung from the cave walls, gently scenting the interior. Tenderly, he led me in, helped me down onto the sheepskins, and lay down beside me. Side by side, we entered the dreamtime. Our dreaming brought our spirits together while he softly taught me to open my soul and merge.

My dream was exciting and encouraging, indicating that I was successfully working on my shamanic task of balancing the male and female aspects of my psyche. I was thrilled to have had such a special, ecstatic dream and to be able to remember it once I awakened. My inner world was clearing and coming more into balance.

My outer world, however, felt like a swamp. Despite all of my good intentions or perhaps because of them, my pain deepened. Being constantly shunned and discounted by Richard was excruciating, and I vacillated between despair, numbed resignation, and unmitigated rage. Within a few days after I had entered the dreamtime with my warrior, I had a dream about Lynn. She was directing me to harden and shine the outer aspects of myself. I saw my exterior as a highly glossed, durable, and sturdy piece of furniture. When I awoke, it was time to call her.

I hadn't spoken with Lynn since August, before my father's surgery and Richard's violent explosion. Now it was December. I wanted to effect some movement in my emotional life and to soothe my pain, but I was ashamed of my part in the drama, and I dreaded telling Lynn about it.

I began our conversation by discussing an incident that had preceded the trauma and had influenced my dreaming. I wanted to start with something relatively benign and work my way up to Richard. "At the end of the summer as I practiced my words of power, I felt a layer of shell or armor fall away from my heart," I told Lynn.

"What was beneath it?" she asked, caught up in the excitement.

"A brilliant gold-white star with a deep blue center. I felt a quietness coming from that center, and I was transported to a still point inside myself. Then the center of my heart opened up."

"Oh, honey, that's beautiful."

"It was clear inside, and the opening felt like a gateway to the universe and to deep space. It was a moment of grace. I'll never forget it. That deep white image stayed with me for days and helped me to connect back to the feelings."

"What about now?"

"My dreaming patterns have changed."

"That's great. If you work on finding your hands in your dreams, it'll increase your dreaming abilities."

"Finding my hands?" I was confused, and I tried to remember if I had ever seen my hands in my dreams before. It seemed familiar, but I had no exact memory of it.

"Yes, find your hands. At first it'll seem like you're going to wake up, but don't let yourself. It will help you in your lucid dreaming."

"What do you mean by lucid dreaming?"

"I mean knowing that you're dreaming while you're still in the dream."

"I think I've done that already." My voice sounded argumentative, and I had a desire to defend my dreaming.

"Just look for your hands," Lynn responded curtly, closing that segment of the conversation. I continued to feel defensive. She went on, definitively changing the subject. "How is your relationship?"

She had done what she always did; she moved straight to the heart of the matter. I recalled her mentioning that when she worked with people over the phone, she had a clearer perspective of the issues because she had to move directly into dreamtime. I wondered if she were looking at my aura and, if so, what she was seeing.

With some degree of hesitation, I began a review. "The last time we talked I was feeling infuriated after I started standing up for myself with Richard. The more I stood up, the angrier I got. Remember?"

"Yes, yes." Lynn's annoyance told me to get to the point.

I shifted the phone to my other ear. I wanted to stall, but I couldn't distract her any longer. I started with the story of my father's surgery and went on to the fight with Richard. I described the events with a sinking heart, wondering what she would say about it. "I was so mad, Lynn, I told him I wanted to kill him. He started telling me how dysfunctional I was, and I told him I wanted to slit his throat." There, it was out. I held my breath, afraid of her response.

Lynn laughed merrily at the other end of the phone, taking me completely by surprise. She didn't consider me vicious after all. A piece of my guilt chipped away. Heartened by her laughter, I continued. "So he decided I was homicidal and dangerous, and he tried to throw me out of the house." I described the whole encounter, including how he had tried to push me down the stairs.

"How awful!" she said.

"He grew up with an alcoholic father. I guess my words reminded him of his childhood."

"Oh, I see. He couldn't help but overreact, given his past. Are you okay? Are you safe now?"

I told Lynn about my Model Mugging classes. She enthusiastically supported my efforts. "That was exactly the right thing to do. Women need to have opportunities to find their voices and to say no."

She continued to comfort and encourage me. I felt

appreciative and quite tearful. I told her about my shame and embarrassment. "You get a gold star, Jennifer. You've done a good job, and you should be proud of yourself. It's despicable how we women always blame ourselves. It wasn't your fault."

I asked Lynn if she had any suggestions about dealing with my continual fury. "When I get mad at Richard, our whole relationship seems to deteriorate. I want to change it, but I don't know what to do."

Her answer was immediate and encouraging. "We all get angry. So what? Anger can be your sword when you feel attacked. It would be nice if we could be calm and have a rational conversation when there are problems, but it isn't always possible."

"If I don't have a way to circumvent my anger, I don't know if I can stay in my marriage."

"Use your anger as a tool for creativity. Sit down and write through it. Feel the anger, and say a prayer. Then take the anger down into your navel, your power center, and begin to work with it."

Relief washed over me as I agreed to try her suggestion, and I thanked her.

"But Jennifer, why didn't you call me when all this happened? Well, you didn't need to. You're building that magnificent power woman inside yourself." She was referring to work we had done together some time ago, toward the beginning of my apprenticeship. I don't remember what we were discussing that preceded the initiation, but Lynn had called forth from within me a certain essence and impeccability, and had introduced her as Power Woman.

"Jennifer," she had said, "move into that place of perfection within you, that place of truth, responsibility, competence, and wisdom. Collect the important parts of yourself, and rid yourself of attitudes not essential to your task. Focus your power on wondrous and magical acts. Follow your innermost passions and manifest your secret dreams. Never seek approval. Approval is based upon doubt. Power lies in your ability to see yourself through your own eyes and not the eyes of another."

Her words had been like arrows perfectly aimed, piercing the obstructions to power in my soul. I still felt Power Woman as a warm current or flow that circulated through me, feeding my strength and sparking my creativity. I called upon her a great deal.

Just before we hung up the phone, Lynn said, "In your aura right now, there is a lot of scar tissue from all the pain you've suffered and you're still feeling. I'll tune in to that in my meditation tonight and help you work with it."

For the next few weeks, each night before I went to sleep, I reminded myself to find my hands in my dreaming. Nothing happened, and I felt frustrated, doubting my abilities. One night while I slept restlessly, I heard a voice commanding me to find my hands. I was aware that I was dreaming. Gathering my intention, I realized I was standing outside the dream, observing. In order to find my hands, I would have to enter the dream consciously so I focused myself and walked into the dream. It felt like I was passing through the gel-like substance of an amoeba, standing inside a living organism. "So this is what it feels like to be inside a dream," I said to myself. I raised my hands to my face and, looking down from my place of witness, I saw the palms of my hands. I turned them back and forth, just to be sure. They were definitely my hands. As I looked them over, I felt a tug to wake up, but remembering Lynn's warning, I held onto my dreamtime awareness.

I was thrilled with my accomplishment and resolved to practice as much as possible. In this tiny glimpse of Lynn's shamanic world, the living quality of the dream felt like an entity in and of itself. Dreaming was not only a vehicle for traveling through the dimensions; it also appeared to be a path toward enlightenment.

I considered the possibilities. I longed to meet with the various women of the Sisterhood of the Shields in my dreaming. In our meditations at Joshua Tree, we often met with some of them for guidance, but this level of dreaming was far more visceral, more intense and multidimensional. Once again, another step along my shamanic path whetted my appetite for more.

# 24

## TRANSITIONS

WINTER AND EARLY SPRING WERE THE DARK SEASONS of my soul. Richard was mostly harsh and unyielding. He interpreted events in his own way, insisting that I agree with his personal worldview in which he felt he was right and everyone else was wrong. Especially me. Depression haunted me while our fights left me wrung out and tearful. I tried to numb myself so I could carry on.

It was New Year's Eve when I made an important resolution to learn detachment. There was no other way. Clearly I needed to stay committed to denying Richard so much influence over my well-being. Lynn had told me that when I learned to stand firm in spite of his moods, I would become a woman of wisdom, no longer at the mercy of other people's whims, distortions, and opinions. Freedom from this tyranny would be my shamanic focus for the new year.

Over the next several months, sometimes I succeeded in remaining detached from my husband's worldview. At other times, when I felt needy or vulnerable, I would fall into a web of intellectualizations and distortions. When I became distraught from not being heard, Richard would call me laughable, suggesting that I look at my issues. Since he felt he was doing nothing to hurt me, he tried to convince me I was doing it to myself. Sometimes I wondered if he were right, and at other times a hot molten fury would boil in my stomach. When this happened, I would fantasize hurting him, and I would dig my nails into my own skin instead of his. Even though I wasn't projecting my anger onto anyone else, this kind of personal rage left me feeling flawed, as if I had some kind of character defect.

I struggled to find emotional ground, aware that my self-esteem was at stake. I was in despair and confusion, and I needed people around me who cared about me and could give me honest feedback about my situation. I turned to some of my women friends, who agreed that not being heard led them to rage, also. Their understanding didn't cool my anger, but I began to see that my extreme feelings were normal. In this way, I slowly began to reclaim my identity and my right to feel my true emotions, whatever they were.

One afternoon when I was alone in the house, I went into a meditation while Gregory napped. I was startled out of the silence by a loud creak on the stairway. In my mind's eye, I saw the image of a large man preparing to attack me. I stiffened in fear and then, reminding myself that I had been trained to fight back, my torso softened, and I relaxed into the vision. The man's skin was black, and light radiated through him, making his flesh shine like highly polished mahogany.

I had seen this vision before, and it had always frightened me, but this time the fear dissolved. I knew that this
luminous figure was not an enemy. Rather, he was a
being of power, and I was uncertain how to proceed.
Lynn once told me that when we are lucky enough to be
confronted by beings of power, we usually become so
overwhelmed and in awe, we overlook the opportunity
before us and forget to ask questions. I decided to ask the
glowing man what to do next. He answered, "Open your
heart and be receptive. Let in my energy."

I breathed deeply, opening as much as possible, and I
was filled with a flood of light and beauty. My insides,
which felt as if they once had been fractured into pieces,
were coming back together. I knew this man represented
a part of my maleness that previously had terrified me.
Now I was able to look at him and see his strength and
beauty. It occurred to me how much of my pain was self-
created, and that the way to freedom was to reintegrate
these fragmented parts of myself. I interpreted my vision
as a medicine sign acknowledging the hard work I was
doing and encouraging me to continue on my path. Perhaps now that I recognized and accepted this male vision
as an ally, I would no longer need to act out negative
male aspects or to allow a man to act them out for me.

The more I worked with my newfound sense of
wholeness, the more I came to realize that I had little or
no power over Richard's actions. Nothing I said or did
seemed to motivate him to take me seriously. He remained unaware of my pain and unconcerned with my

needs. I wondered if he were trying to run me out of the relationship by discounting my presence. I recognized that his lack of love for me was not the problem; it was his fear of love itself. It seemed that loving anyone outside himself threatened his sense of security. This was clearly demonstrated during one of our therapy sessions when Larry said to Richard, "If you cannot stop blaming this woman, you're going to ruin your marriage. Can you stop blaming her?"

"No" was Richard's answer.

It was after my vision of the luminous male that something new emerged. A profound peacefulness would suddenly appear, sometimes the ease welling up from a quiet place within, sometimes washing over me from the outside. When this happened, it remained with me throughout the rest of the day, and I knew my spirit was deepening. I attributed my newfound peace to my psychological work combined with my connection to Agnes Whistling Elk and the Sisterhood of the Shields. It was during these days in the calm of my introspection that I began to prepare myself for a new possibility: leaving my marriage. It was either that or suffer the continuing devastation of my spirit.

My support system of women friends was my haven. They reinforced my sanity by reminding me that no matter what Richard said, I was a warm, caring woman, deserving of great love. "Other people are kind and loving with me," I told Richard in the middle of one of his critical tangents. "They tell me I am worthwhile and wise. Why don't you?"

"Those people love you because they don't have to live with you, Jennifer. If they knew you like I did, they'd be singing a different tune."

I knew he was being mean, but the doubt was still there. I often felt unlovable, and the more I heard him say it, the harder it was to counteract.

When Richard's character attacks went on too long, I lapsed into silence. For him, my quiet times must have been a relief as he could go for weeks without speaking to me except for an occasional comment about something practical or logistical. He seemed peaceful when I was silent, oblivious to my discomfort, my anger, or my frustration. He would get up in the mornings and play with Gregory as if I didn't exist. I wondered if he would care or even notice if I left.

One night in the stillness of my meditation, I knew it was over. I felt dead and beaten down, unappreciated by my husband and unwelcome in my own home. I had to go. Being on my own without my husband was the only way I would come alive again.

This was the end and the beginning. I prepared myself to live the life of a single woman raising a child, the very thing I had dreaded for so long.

# 25

## THE ANGER DOLL

"OF COURSE YOU'RE ANGRY. WHAT HAPPENED WAS unfair, and you were treated poorly," Lynn told me. I was at her house in Los Angeles two weeks after I left Richard. "But now, we need to get that anger out of you. There is so much darkness out there in the world right now, and while you need to go through this negativity, you don't want to attract more. I want you to be careful."

"That scares me," I said. Pale and tense, I sat on the edge of her sofa, searching my teacher's face for solace, comfort, the doorway beyond my grief.

"Nonsense," replied Lynn. "There's nothing to fear. You simply need to take control of your destiny and manage the situation. You'll be fine. Now start at the beginning and tell me everything."

I filled her in on my decision to leave and my feelings throughout the various stages that led to my leaving. "The day of the move was filled with drama. I decided to do it without his knowing because I was afraid of his violence."

"That was wise," Lynn assured me.

"Richard left for an early appointment that morning. He had a lunch date, and the movers were scheduled to arrive at noon. There was a misunderstanding, and the movers almost couldn't make it. The owner of the company ended up coming over himself at the last minute. While we were packing up the boxes, I heard a message on the machine for Richard. It was his lunch date, canceling. I knew he'd be home before I was gone."

"What did you do?" Lynn asked, concern clouding her face.

"Bonnie was there, and she decided to take Gregory, go to my new apartment, and let me finish up with the movers. I was frightened, especially when Richard showed up just as the workers were closing up the van. Bonnie saw him first when she was halfway down the driveway. She shouted back to me to leave right away.

"I managed to back my car in between Richard's car and the van. I could see his face; it was red with rage. He gunned his car forward to block my way, but I squeezed through." I shook my shoulders to relieve the tension.

"What you have done is an act of power," Lynn declared. "To continue the resolution on this, I think you should make an anger doll about the relationship. The left side is feminine, the right side masculine. The body of your doll is your feelings, and the appendages represent Richard. The head is spirit."

I groaned inwardly. Not another doll.

Lynn went on, unaware of my resistance or maybe just ignoring it. "I want you to get a punching bag or something like it, anything that makes noise when you hit it. Agnes says the noise is important for purifying anger out of the body's central nervous system. See your anger flowing from your body like a dirty brown river flows into the earth. Give your anger to Mother Earth. She knows how to handle it better than we do; she is enormously wise."

I nodded, in agreement with Lynn's belief that the earth is alive and filled with power and wisdom.

"Another way to transform anger is through writing, Jennifer. Take that energy and put it back into the work you're doing. Use it creatively, and one day, you'll notice it's gone."

"Oh, Lynn," I groaned. "I'm so tired. It feels like everything takes so much effort. I just can't get out from under it, and I can't see past this heavy stage. Will I ever have something fun to look forward to? Right now, it's all work."

"I know how you feel. There are times like that, and you're in one, but if you could see how many spirits are gathered around you that want to help, you'd feel easier. They want you to be comfortable, but they are spirits of light and they can't get through to you until you release the dense vibrations that surround you. Let's do a little work with this right now. Close your eyes."

I sank back into the now-familiar sofa and closed my eyes, hoping that Lynn might be able to help. I felt the heaviness around me; I just didn't know how to get past it. I softened as much as possible and focused on Lynn's voice. "Imagine the shining sun, radiant and golden. Slowly perceive the sun coming toward you. Feel the warmth. It's a little bit too hot to be comfortable. Feel the heat at the top of your head as it enters your crown chakra at the center of your head. As the heat moves through you, it burns away fear, pain, and addictions."

I clearly could see the sun, and each time it touched my pain, a bright fizzle of light flashed like a sparkler on the fourth of July. The light show of sparks showered and arched into nothingness. Then I felt the sun settle in the base of my spine, spinning quickly to the right. A ruby red brilliance began to form around the sun wheel, looking like a ring of jewels melding into one large circle and shooting fire from the center. I heard Lynn's voice as if from far away.

"See the wheel turning to the right," she said. "Many people have imbalances in their energy centers causing them to spin counterclockwise. Stress, anger, fear, or even a bad dream can cause the energy to turn to the left. Then it can't move up your spine properly. Take some time and focus on your circle moving clockwise to the right."

I took several deep breaths as the wheel continued spinning to the right with extraordinary speed.

"Now focus on the center of the disk. To the left of center, see an old woman with long gray braids. See her dancing in place, expressing joy, passion, and love of life. Her movements are simple and graceful, her posture strong and proud. She is your elder guardian and has been with you for a very long time. Look into her eyes. She has a message for you about how to make your life magical."

My guardian was wearing a red leather dress with fringes hanging from her arms and the hem of her skirt. Although she was old, her movements were fluid and vital like those of a younger woman. Her eyes shone with passion and intensity; her focus upon me held me motionless.

She spoke. "When you let out the love that is inside you, then the magic is possible. Bring home the beauty in nature; it will heal you and offer you the solace that you need."

She looked toward the center of the circle, and my eyes followed hers. There stood an old man in native dress, proud and handsome, dancing in the ancient way of the Indians. He was stately in stature, he looked clear and grounded, and he gave off a sense of kindness, intelligence, and humor. His nature did not come across as aggressive, but for some reason, I was too frightened to make out his words. I strained to hear him above my internal noise. Lynn's voice interrupted my struggle. I thought she was about to rescue me by interpreting his words, which I could not understand, but as usual, she was not about to do the work for me; she wanted to empower me to do it for myself. "This man loves you very much," she said. "He has a message for you about magic. Look him in the eye, and try to hear him now."

I would have to pass through my fear and get the message for myself. I still felt afraid, but Lynn's words had

soothed me. I plucked up my courage and focused on the
fierce kindness in the old man's face. It was true; he did
love me. Slowly my fear subsided, and I began to make
out his words. "Whether you know it or not, it is magic
that sustains you in your work and your relationships. You
have done a good job."

I smiled. I didn't have to go looking for the magic; it
was already here. I simply had to recognize it. The elders
turned toward each other and embraced. Light and flames
engulfed them as they gently dissolved from sight. Lynn
spoke. "They are burning with the fire of love and passion. Feel the balance of their energies inside you as you
begin to move the sun up your body and out into the
universe."

I felt the heat scald me as it rose up through my entire
body and filtered out into the ethers above my head. I sat
back, exhausted. Lynn's eyes were bright. "Jennifer, practice this meditation every day. It will help you. The beings
on the other side who love you will be able to send their
love and support to you more easily as a result of the
lightness this will bring to you."

I drove home on fire. I could hardly wait to see my
elders again and work with them. I would have liked to
skip the punching bag and just do the meditation, but I
knew better. The very next day, I went out and bought a
blow-up bozo doll in place of a punching bag. He looked
like a referee, dressed in black-and-white stripes, and after
the initial resistance wore off, I decided it wasn't such a
bad thing to have a life-size doll to punch around. Since

Gregory was visiting with his father for the afternoon, I stood the doll in the middle of the living room, swore at it, and gave it a good kick. It felt good and I kicked it again. The next thing I knew, I was kicking and shoving the doll toward the doorway and chasing it down the hall. When poor old Bozo ended up at the entrance to my bedroom, I reached back my arm and swung at it with all my might. When my fist connected with its plastic body, it flew across the entire length of the room and sailed into the nightstand. I watched in amazement as the doll hit the lamp with enough force to send it crashing through the bedroom window, leaving large glass shards on the floor.

I stared at the gaping hole in the window. And still, the anger hadn't left. I remembered the cassette tape by death and dying expert, Elisabeth Kübler-Ross, who talked about the importance of externalizing rage by hitting a rubber hose against a phone book. As if possessed, I grabbed a couple of phone books and ran outside to the porch. I dropped the phone books by my feet, swung the garden hose, and heard a satisfying thunk. I hit the phone books again and again until my arms and shoulders ached. When I was thoroughly exhausted, I dropped the hose, fell to the ground, and cried. Huge shuddering sobs racked their way through my body, and I cried for my lost dreams. Eventually the torrent subsided and a quiet descended upon me. I experienced a moment of peace that made me feel grateful.

A few days later, I made my anger doll. I twisted a wire hanger into a facsimile of a body and wrapped red and black yarn around it until it was plump. Her head hung over to one side, and try as I might, I couldn't make it stand up straight on her wire shoulders. Her slumped head gave her a defeated appearance while the contrast of red against black hooked into my feelings of rage. I placed her on my altar and meditated with her, inviting her to draw out my repressed feelings.

After many days, my anger gradually began to ease, and I noticed that my heart felt lighter. It surprised me that as I grieved the loss of my lifelong dream, at the same time I often felt buoyant and delighted with life. In a private therapy session with Larry, I told him I had left the relationship.

"Your presence feels much healthier. Good for you," he commented.

Lynn had also mentioned how much healthier I looked. Larry worked with me during the session to find another crucial piece of myself that had been missing. "Go into the sadness you spoke about earlier," he encouraged. "Tell me what you find."

I paused, closed my eyes, and focused on my feelings. Scattered around the sadness were self-accusatory messages, such as, "It's my fault. I'm not good enough. I should have tried harder." I spoke them out loud, and Larry continued to guide me.

"I want you to move into your healthy part. From that place of clarity and truth, speak to those negative thoughts."

I did as he suggested. I told the thoughts that they weren't accurate, and they weren't mine. They were simply inherited messages that were about to change. The negativity was no longer deeply rooted. As I countered each negative message with life-enhancing truth and reality, I felt relieved. My commitment was to love and beauty and to transforming the grief into creativity.

When the session was over, Larry said, "I want you to practice directness. Whenever you hear that internal negativity, whether it's Richard's voice or an old societal voice, remember to pause, move into the healthy part of yourself, and confront those voices from your strength, clarity, and truth."

We hugged good-bye. This time my tears were not about sadness but rather gratitude. I was walking away with yet another piece to the puzzle of my wholeness.

# 26

## GRIEVING AND GRACE

I ALTERNATED BETWEEN RELIEF AND DISTRESS AT MY new life circumstances. In an attempt to gather my serenity, I often sat on my new back porch. There I watched the sun filter through the sheltering pine tree, creating a lacy border of shadow on my small patch of grass. One summer afternoon as I reclined on my deck chair, drifting along the border of sleep and awareness, I had a vision.

"Why don't you try softening around your discomfort?" an inner voice suggested.

Why not? I breathed deeply and settled into the physical soreness that surrounded my heart. With the next deep breath, I relaxed into the pain, and the image of my inner woman came to me. She was bloodied and bruised, and her clothes were in tatters. I knew she was having difficulty, but I was surprised by how battered she was. I spoke to her in soft tones; then I undressed her and examined her wounds. The damage was too extensive for a mere topical potion. A deep healing balm was necessary.

This vision was occurring in another time and dimension, so healing could be immediate. In my mind, I invented a bath filled with an aloe vera–like substance. As I carefully washed the inner feminine aspect of myself, her bruises and cuts disappeared as if by magic. I washed and combed her hair, all the while speaking in soothing tones about how much I loved her and how important she was to me. I invited her inner power and potency to return. Then I dried her off, dressed her in a soft buckskin dress, and called in Lynn's teachers, Agnes and Ruby. I presented her to them and asked them to help my woman heal into the next stages of growth and beauty.

They accepted her gladly, greeting her with warmth. "We, your sisters, are here for you." I promised my inner woman that I would meet with her again very soon. The vision shifted and my inner eye was filled with past images of Richard and myself in conflict. He suddenly metamorphosed into a gigantic red and green monster with swollen bubbles and scratchy scales all over his skin. His energy was enormous; it flattened me onto the ground and I could barely move. Helpless beneath him, I was covered with a layer of his red and green scales as he walked over me. In terror, I called out to Lynn. She appeared before me in a soft yellow glow. Her face floated in front of me, surrounded by a yellowish halo.

"Get up," she said. "Stand on your two feet."

The power of her words propelled me to my feet, and there I stood with a sword in my hand. I let out a cry like a screaming banshee and ran forward, piercing the monster with my sword, impaling him to the ground. A crack formed in the earth, and the ghastly mutant began dissolving into the ground. When there was not even a trace of him left, I knew that the earth had cleansed and transformed him. The crevice deepened, and I began softly traveling down a tunnel into the cool, soothing atmosphere of the earth.

A light in the distance beckoned me forward. I passed through it to find myself standing in a cavern. It was completely still. Oruncha, a powerful sky being, awaited me. An aboriginal ancestor warrior, he stood tall and bearded. Geometric designs of red and white ochre covered his body, suggesting his ceremonial intent. I greeted him with enthusiasm. I trusted him; we had met several years before, during one of my earliest initiations with Lynn.

Oruncha guided me to the middle of the cavern where a platform had been set into the ground, reflecting a ruby light that emanated from the center of the earth. I lay on the platform while Oruncha encouraged me to use my feminine powers to become receptive to nourishment from the earth. Flashes of crystal clear water, pine forest, bay trees, and the fecundity of the forest floor penetrated me. I felt instantly refreshed.

Before I left the cavern, Oruncha implanted optically clear diamond chunks into various transmission points of my body. I knew these gems would act as windows to higher consciousness, repelling negativity. He showed me a massive quartz crystal the size of a mountain, inviting me to step into this crystalline environment. I walked straight into the white, hot brilliance, shimmering with rainbows. Bubbles of light floated around my head, and I saw cracks in the crystal walls, beckoning me with the promise of other worlds. I wanted to jump in, but I stayed where I was, in the center of the activity. The multifaceted diamonds he had placed in my body began vibrating as if with song, resonating to the pristine and charismatic light of the crystal. I shivered as visions of imploding and exploding points of light danced and swirled through me. From this vantage point, Oruncha taught me about balancing my male/female aspects. The clarity of my crystalline container represented the perfection of receptivity. It was the most potent kind of teaching, that of direct experience.

Early the next morning, I was awakened by an image of a white tourbillion, a spiral vortex of energy. I was being drawn into the center of the swirling force, and I felt scared. I struggled to open my eyes, hoping that if I did, the image would fade. But even with my eyes open, I was still being drawn inward. I was heading for the center of that vortex; I tried to resist and then realized that I had no choice but to relax as best I could and go with it. I surrendered, picking up extraordinary speed, and landed with a jolt on the other side of a brilliant white light.

A woman stood in front of me, beaming with radiance and clarity, greeting me by vibrating the cells of my body. I thought she must have been an angel or a fairy. She seemed to be constructed from transparent layers of light, and there was a sense of a yielding to her, a softness that blurred the edges of her form. She shimmered with electricity, and when I focused on any particular part of her form, currents of energy passed through me. She was like nothing I had ever seen, either in person or in spirit, and I blinked my eyes several times, wondering if she were really there.

"You are granted one wish," she communicated in her wordless fashion. I thought I heard a cascade of bells behind her, similar to the sounds I heard when Lynn was leading me into an altered state.

I stood dumbfounded for a moment, and then as if someone were encouraging me to speak, I told her, "I want a healthy loving family with Gregory, a loving mate, and any other children we might conceive."

"So it is," she told me. My mind snapped back, and I was lying in my bed, wide awake.

I got out of bed and tiptoed into Gregory's room, and watched him sleep for a moment. Then I moved into the kitchen with a mission. I wanted to fashion Fairy Woman in the form of a doll, so that I might stay connected with her. I took a roll of saran wrap, and pulled out layers upon layers, shaping arms and legs attached to a plastic torso. When I was finished, I placed her in the part of my altar that was devoted to spirit.

The first time I prayed to Fairy Woman before I went to bed, my inner child's heart whispered, "I wonder if she is real. Is it possible that she would make our wish come true?"

I held my special pillow to my stomach and comforted her. "Yes," I said. "It's possible." And we both dropped off to sleep.

# 27

## THE SACRED WOMB

THE CLOSE OF MY NORTHERN YEAR PRESENTED me with a difficult choice. I was preparing to go to the yearly gathering with Lynn, and I had to decide what to do with Gregory. He was fifteen months old, and we never had been separated for more than a few hours. I hated the idea of leaving him. At the same time, I badly needed a break. When I thought about having him in Joshua Tree, I couldn't face the ever-increasing demands of mothering combined with the fully packed day-and-night schedule of the medicine retreat. But could I trust leaving Gregory with his father? Richard was willing to take him, but he had never been responsible for Gregory for extended time periods. And yet, I was depleted and needed to replenish myself. The debate went on until I finally made my decision. Richard would take Gregory for the four days. Despite whatever had gone on between the two of us, when Richard was one on one with his son, he had shown up as a responsible and caring father.

The night before the gathering, I sat in my motel room and wept as if my heart were breaking. I must have made a mistake leaving my son, I thought. What if he needs me?

I eventually dropped off to sleep, calmed by my sobs, finding a small part of me that was relieved to be alone.

The first day of the retreat, I was mortified to notice that my internal voice was booming out negative messages. I looked at the other women with a critical eye, and I was angry. I tried to focus on positive thoughts, but I just couldn't seem to muster them. I was sure that everybody else was having beautiful spiritual moments while I was confronting my inner ugliness.

Lynn, in her infinite wisdom and insight, spoke to this issue on the first night. "Have you ever noticed that when someone, a woman in particular, does an extraordinary act and rises above the crowd, people will begin to dislike her or criticize her? No matter who she is, there always will be a chink in the armor, something that isn't perfect. You can find it if you look. But it's so destructive to focus on the negative in one of your sisters instead of the positive. It stems from insecurity, and I'm asking all of you to be aware of this tendency. Do your best to stop this in yourselves."

I was embarrassed, as if she had been speaking directly to me. Had my energy field reflected this kind of objectionable behavior? Or was it a tendency for everyone? Lynn continued to discuss this topic. "There are entities that live off of negative thought forms. When you have these kinds of thoughts, it's as if you're feeding them a big, juicy steak." Nervous laughter swept through the room. I winced as I imagined dark energy forms sucking out my life force.

From her chair, Lynn held up one hand with her palm facing us. "Really, I know it sounds funny, but I'm serious. Each time you indulge in this, you're feeding these entities. Please be aware."

Although some part of me felt ashamed and exposed, I was glad Lynn had spoken about this phenomenon. Now that she had reminded me that my unpleasant thoughts were stemming from my own insecurity, I could work with them. This was my next personal task: catching the negativity and rerouting my attention to unearth the fear and insecurity. I was rewarded with immediate results; the next day was much more comfortable. I craved the peacefulness the way a parched desert rat needs a drink of water.

The focus of this year's retreat was to create a ceremonial gourd. "Gourds represent the new womb for seeding and creating magic," Lynn explained. "For many years, we have been looking inward, going into our self-wounds to find the seeds of enlightenment. It has been a process of implosion. It is essential that we balance this inward journey with an outward explosion of energy. Then we can connect with our own 'wombness' and, through the magic of the gourd, create our life anew."

Celebration of accomplishments big and small was the focus of the work as we prepared to paint our gourds, bless them, and include them in our array of sacred power objects. My past year had been filled with pain, battling, and isolation. It seemed that I had little to celebrate at present, so I placed my attention on the little joys that I found from day to day. My gratitude and connection to the smaller things helped to heal the grief of the separation. I prayed that I might move into harmony with all of life and to live within the center of my being. I also prayed for the strength to release the hostility that pervaded my thoughts.

Three hundred women who were grouped together, opening their hearts and painting their sacred gourds, were a powerful sight to behold. It was a great honor to be among them. The colors of the paints ranged from brilliant reds and oranges to neon purples to subtle blues and greens. While we involved ourselves in the physical task of adorning our gourds with feathers, crystals, and various specimens from nature, we prayed, cleansed, meditated, and cared for ourselves and one another. As always, the work with Lynn was concerned with maintaining balance of the whole by nurturing and attending to our physical, emotional, and spiritual aspects.

When our sacred works of art were prepared, we gathered in the large meeting hall. It was time to contact the sacred keeper of the gourds. Lynn guided us into the meditation by creating a calm within which we could access a heightened dimension. Once we had entered into the harmony, Gourd Woman emerged from out of the whiteness of the moon. She was an ancient-looking figure, dressed in bright red with a beaded red shield around her neck.

"Gourd Woman is keeper of the sacred gourds," Lynn told us. "Look into her face; see her merriment and joy.

See the quality of depth in her eyes. She holds a sense of direction, of possibility, of hope. See her abiding understanding of character. She knows exactly who she is. Perhaps you hope to be like her. Look into her eyes, holding with her the sacred void that represents the emptiness and the magic of the universe. All of this is contained within a single gourd, a magnificent and perfect creation of earth and spirit that comes from a single seed, planted in Mother Earth. Here you can contemplate the goodness of your lives. Be open to whatever life has to give you."

Gourd Woman took over, guiding us in building our personal gourd garden. Mine was a desert oasis, spotted with saguaro cactus, Joshua trees, and other desert brush plants. Water bubbled from a spring, and tiny white flowers with yellow centers and fragile green stems, sparse but fragrant, grew out of the rocks surrounding the spring. Desert cedar trees surrounded the area, their sparse branches and needles creating shadow play with the sunlight. This garden, alive and fertile, seemed to exist not only outside of me in its natural desert environment, but inside of me as well. It was my inner gourd womb of creativity.

The highlight of the second day was a movement meditation in which I imagined my body to be a seed-pod. I curled up in the smallest possible form, and Lynn guided us through the seasons of our lives. I felt my breath and awareness expand as I evolved from a tiny pod to a sprouting stem to a tall supple tree and back to the earth once again. My fears of death were suspended;

I appreciated each magnificent and diverse stage of life. I fell into bed just before midnight where the evolution of my plant life continued into my dreams.

We spent a good part of the third day exploring personal freedoms and the blocks that kept us from them. I knew this ceremony would allow me to assess my contribution to the difficulties in my marriage, as well as to release more grief and disappointment. Joined together with a partner, we walked out into the desert to set up a medicine circle representing power and self-worth. I chose Laura, an athletic-looking woman in her sixties, to be my partner. Her white hair was pulled back into a ponytail exposing her wide open eyes and the kindness in her face. Her muscles were wiry and strongly developed, and she carried a fierceness of spirit, as if long, enduring battles had shaped her both physically and spiritually. I admired her strength and directness, qualities I wished to embody.

Laura and I found our sacred spot. We began the ceremony by burning sage and choosing a stone for each of the four directions. When the wheel was complete, I started my dance along the inside of the wheel as my partner moved in tandem with me along the outside. Facing the south, which represents the physical world, we followed Lynn's instructions to think about our relationship to beauty, money, and fulfillment as associated with friends, acts of power, vocations, and social life.

"For the last two years, during my marriage to Richard," I told my partner, "I lost my connection to beauty both within myself and in the outer world." Tears soaked my face, softening the lines of worry and pain, and I did nothing to stop them. "Many friends fell away from my life during this time, and my business diminished, partly due to my commitment to my son, but also due to my lack of faith in my skills and abilities. I was so lost, I often worked by rote. Now I need to recapture the heart and meaning in my work with people because this is the work that I love."

I felt shattered. My life lay in fragments before me, and I put my head in my hands and sobbed. Laura did nothing to interfere; she stayed with me in her unfaltering and nonjudgmental gaze, witnessing my destruction, willing to be there for my resurrection. After what seemed like hours, although perhaps it was only moments, the torrent subsided. I spoke with clarity directly to Laura. "I need commitment. From this moment forward, I commit myself to gathering my abilities to recreate my life with beauty."

I walked to the west. I sat while Laura mirrored me by sitting and facing me. I stayed silent until serenity emerged. "During my marriage, I used my doubt and confusion as a veil to obscure my vision of what was real. I relied on my husband's vision. However accurate or inaccurate it was for him, it was not right for me. In this way, I forfeited my dreams and began to slowly die. Through the teachings of silence in the west, I resolve to live again, to move beyond my doubts, confusion, and pain to reclaim my power."

Laura smiled broadly and released an emphatic shout of agreement.

I moved to the north. "Laura, my husband has been a teacher for me. If he was able to get inside my head and confuse me, then I needed to make some changes. I had to find out how to live my own reality, and that took strength. It was through knowing him and leaving him that I built that kind of strength. I never will have to go through another experience like that again because I'll recognize it before it happens."

I walked into the east, ready to confront the truth. "Here in the east, I can see that not only did I deceive myself, but I also deceived Richard. I acted wishy-washy. I let him think of me as more pliable than I really was. My deception became a trap for me, and I got caught in the web of deceit. It was a terrible experience for both of us."

Lightness bubbled up from somewhere inside and, with Laura echoing my spontaneous laughter, I saw clearly how I had chosen my illusions and Richard had chosen his. "From now on, I will use my imagination not to deceive myself, but rather to create my destiny."

Laura and I hugged each other briefly before she took her place in the center of the wheel of self-worth. I moved to the outside to become witness to her journey around the circle.

On the last night of the retreat, forty-four of us were honored with the gift of a red ribbon for attending four years of Whistling Elk gatherings. When Lynn gave me my ribbon, she hugged me with warmth and strength.

Her final words to the entire group were a reminder about the importance of redirecting our negative thoughts, the theme she had introduced at the beginning, which now seemed like a lifetime ago.

"When you are talking with a friend and tear someone else down, you are hurting everyone, yourself included. The negativity floats around in your presence, undoing all the hard work you have accomplished. Learn to stop it now."

Her voice was emphatic. I knew that negativity had been a constant companion in my life. It would take discipline and commitment to make the shift. I made the commitment. I wanted to live a good and useful life, I wanted to be happy, I wanted to know the magic of existence, and I wanted that for my son.

I left Joshua Tree with a lighter heart, prepared to begin again. I was raising my son on my own, recreating my life. I was refreshed and enthusiastic, ready to take action, aware of the inevitable obstacles and future trials, and at the same time strengthened by the taste of freedom and the promise of power, willing to face whatever lay ahead. I felt the irresistible magnetic force of the Great Mystery, the pull of the Sacred Void. I heard the call to joy and celebration along my path. I answered. I said yes, now and forever.

# EPILOGUE

I AM HOVERING BETWEEN WAKING AND SLEEPING, IN my own center and also that of dreamtime. I am soothed by the flow of warm water covering the ground, as I sit with my back toward a rocky cavern. I feel the draw of the void and turn to face it. I am compelled to pass through the opening, but first, I must climb the slick, mossy rocks in order to enter into the depths of the interior. Into the depths of my own interior.

Once in the center of the void, I sense a presence. I turn toward it, facing the wall where a ledge juts out. I see a large gold and black bee, the goddess's emissary. Power beckons. Doubt. Fear. I retreat from the cave, afraid that I have trespassed. The bee follows, buzzing persistently around my body.

It stings me hard on my right leg, and I swat at it. Stunned, it falls to the ground. I step on it with all my weight, deliberately killing it, and then realizing its connection to all other bees, to the rest of its species. It is dead, but the others are very much alive and I foresee that, soon, I will be swarming with bees, wearing them like a writhing, stinging gold and black coat. I see them on my arms and legs, filling my mouth and ears.

"Agnes, Lynn, women from the Sisterhood," I call out. "Help me."

Lynn's voice comes to me. "Go back to the ledge and make an offering."

The idea is fearsome to me, and I am sure I have nothing to offer. I look down at my hand; it is oozing with honey, as are my arms, my belly, my breasts. The roof of my mouth and tongue are melting into honey as well, sweetness seeping from my pores. I fill a plate with sage, cedar, tobacco, sweetgrass, crystals, and cornmeal. I take it into the cavern, setting my offering on the ledge, allowing the honey to drip from every part of my body and trail through the cavern. Remorse from my heart. Food for the bees.

Lights dance around me; color plays off of the walls. From within the depths of the cavern, luminous golden threads angle across each other, forming an intricate web of silken brilliance. The face of the goddess appears amid the shifting, pulsating shapes. She has accepted my offering. Watching the radiance burst around me like a cosmic sparkler, I will myself into the center of the light. Standing at the hub of the wheel of life, I watch as my personal history plays itself out in images amid the shining spokes of gold.

I see the child I was three years prior, struggling to meet the moment-to-moment demands of growing and becoming a woman of power. Her arms are outstretched, and as I reach out to embrace her, a great keening fills the air. It is the eerie sound of her grief and longing to come home. Slivery thin tendrils of golden light reach out from my hands, and I pull her to me. I am the Corn Mother, welcoming my child back to the nest. I open my mouth and croon reassuring melodies that speak to her doubts and soothe her pain. Her sorrows are mine and so are her dreams of joy. I accept all that she is. She dissolves into my body, and we are one.

# ABOUT THE AUTHOR

JENNIFER MORSE, M.S., M.F.C.C., IS A LICENSED MARRIAGE and family therapist who combines her traditional therapeutic skills with the ceremony and wisdom she has learned in apprenticeship with Lynn V. Andrews and the shamanic teachings of the Sisterhood of the Shields. She spins this living legacy into the weavings of an ordinary life, offering the potential for transformation for herself and others. Jennifer divides her time between continuing her apprenticeship with Lynn and the Center for Shamanic Arts, working with clients, writing, and applying the wisdom gathered on her journey to daily life in order to touch the world with beauty.

If you are interested in further information regarding work with Jennifer, you may contact her at:

Jennifer Morse
177 Alice Avenue
Campbell, CA 95008
(408) 379-3839

The publisher offers:

Walk in Spirit:
Prayers for the Seasons of Life
*by Lynn V. Andrews*

The Bliss of Freedom
*by Master Charles*

The Mask of Power
*by Lynn V. Andrews*

The Practical Wisdom Audio Tape Series
*by Lynn V. Andrews*

Acacia Publishing Corporation
23852 Pacific Coast Highway, Suite 756
Malibu, CA 90265

Please write us at the above address
if you wish to be added to our mailing list.

ACACIA

PUBLISHING
CORPORATION

*Transforming the World, One Page at a Time...*